WHERE TRUE LOVE IS

An Affirming Devotional for LGBTQI+
Christians and Their Allies

SUZANNE DeWITT HALL

Foreword by

SUSAN COTTRELL

Author of *Mom, I'm Gay* and *True Colors.*

Cover photograph courtesy of Tetyana Afanasyeva/Shutterstock.

DH Strategies
www.ipromotebooks.com

First Edition
Revision 2.0

ISBN-13: 978-0-9864080-2-1
ISBN-10: 0-9864080-2-6

Printed in the United States of America

DEDICATION

Jesus Christ was sent to correct our wildly inaccurate understanding of God. If we pay attention, we discover that our creator continues to use this strategy in the lives of Christians today, sending us people who shine the light of Jesus so brightly and in such unexpected ways that we are momentarily blinded and baffled. Encountering them forces us to evaluate everything we thought about our faith.

Diane DeWitt Hall is a beautiful example of this incarnational theophany. She stepped in to my Bible study one morning and my life and faith were forever transformed.

This devotional is the fruit of our subsequent years of scriptural examination, contemplation, and discussion. If Diane hadn't had the courage to say yes to God and to me, the book would not exist.

Thank you for all your yeses, my Dolce. I love you, into eternity.

CONTENTS

FOREWORD

BY SUSAN COTTRELL, AUTHOR OF *MOM, I'M GAY* AND
TRUE COLORS

Suzanne DeWitt has written a delightful and dexterous devotional, *Where True Love Is!* She is a magician who shows us an empty square of cloth, ties it then unties it, to reveal a dove within! The empty cloth is our understanding of Correct Doctrine, which Suzanne ties and unties to reveal the Holy Spirit within!

Page after page, I smiled and highlighted Suzanne's insights. For example:

> *"Let's look at John's wonderful proclamation again: 'Everyone who loves has been born of God and knows God.' What a powerfully inclusive statement."*

Powerfully inclusive indeed, and at direct odds with the exclusivity of so much of conservative Christian teaching, especially as they relate to the LGBTQI+ community.

Suzanne takes us on a journey to see God, the Bible, and Jesus as never before. She reminds us about God: "John doesn't say 'God is loving.' He says 'God is love.' That's a world of difference." She tells us that the *Holy Spirit* breathes life, not the Bible.

She shows Jesus as lawbreaker who *defends* breaking the law, but also *fulfills* the law—and why that's important for us! For those who've been run over by a truck of misused Bible passages, this devotional is healing.

Suzanne deals directly with homophobia, as when she talks about the woman who broke several commands as she touched Jesus' robe:

> *"It was not her fault she had been bleeding for years. It was governed by some internal mystery of organs and hormones, and was not fixable despite her efforts to try and change it. The same thing is true for LGBTQI+ people. Their gender and sexual orientation is not something controllable or chosen. It cannot be "fixed" through conversion therapy or stern biblical admonitions. It simply is. These people should not be confined to closets as this woman with the issue of blood had been.*
>
> *It was not her strict adherence to the rites and rituals of religion which made her whole. It was her faith. And that faith allowed her to go in peace."*

If you are looking for an enlightening perspective—if you want encouragement instead of discouragement—this is the devotional for you.

Enjoy every page: I did!

INTRODUCTION

Can you be gay or transgender and Christian?

The answer is yes.

If you identify as gay, lesbian, bisexual, transgender, intersex, queer, or any other designation; welcome. If you love someone who identifies as one of those designations; welcome. In this space you are safe. In this space you are recognized as a particular expression of the image and likeness of God. In this space you can experience wholeness as a follower of Christ.

As a member of your community and an ally, I've heard your stories. Jamie was kicked out of his house as a teenager when his mother found out he was gay. Allen lost his job teaching at a Christian college when he announced he was transitioning. Kim stopped going to church when her son came out, because she only heard words of condemnation there and couldn't line up their statements with the reality of her beloved child. Kathy was told she couldn't come to church wearing women's clothes. These are true stories told with heartbroken voices, and they are just a handful of thousands of examples. Perhaps millions.

In many of these stories, the protagonist dies. Some are murdered by people who consider them subhuman or evil. Others commit suicide, overcome by the ugliness they face, and unable to stand a future of more.

Meanwhile, Jesus weeps.

In 2008 I began writing about the way our souls hunger for God, in a blog titled *A Theology of Desire*. At that time I was desperately lonely and struggling to keep my unhappy marriage afloat. I was completely submitted to the idea of Until Death do Us Part, and hoped for an early demise. Exploring the intersection of sexuality and Catholic theology kept me alive, and provided an outlet for my spirit's raging demand for love.

But God, in his mercy, had other plans.

Into church one day walked a Baptist woman named Diane who would eventually become my wife. She was at a crossroads in her own marriage, though I wouldn't know that for another few years. She began attending my weekly Bible study, where we prayed together for our husbands and families. We desired obedience to God's will, with our church's assurance that if we were Proverbs 31 wives, our men could surely become Ephesians 5 husbands. But as we continued to study the word of God and share our lives together, we realized no matter how hard you Proverbs 31, you can't make someone else change. And as we became increasingly closer— laughing, crying, working for the church, and praying together— something inexplicable happened. We fell in love.

This was a pretty big deal given that our Christian foundations, while completely different, were both adamantly opposed to same-sex relationships. It was an even bigger deal for our socially conservative church. As our marriages went through their final death throes, the priest and his all-male rector's council was at a loss about what to do with us. We were eventually asked to stop attending so we wouldn't cause "confusion" amongst the body. It was ugly and painful, and the memories still hurt.

Our story is far from unique, and we were the lucky ones; we had each other. Many people aren't as fortunate.

Diane and I come to the LGBTQI+ table in a unique way. We identify as heterosexual by base orientation, and yet are deeply, completely, and eternally in love. Together with God we are a cord of three strands which cannot be broken. Every day we commit to putting God first, each other second, and everything else in proper order after that. Every day we agree to submit to God's will for our lives together, and seek his guidance over all our work. That is what Christian marriage is all about, and that is what we desire for all of God's people, regardless of sexual orientation or gender identity.

This book is for every LGBTQI+ individual who fears God can't love them just the way they are, and for those who simply want a devotional which approaches scripture inclusively. It is for every family member who struggles to integrate the reality of their LGBTQI+ loved one with a faithful walk with Christ. It is for every pastor, church, and denomination trying to discern God's will for this critical issue.

My hope is that by pondering each day's page, you will receive peace and comfort from the God who loves you, and that by the end of our 90 days together, you will be equipped to defend the right of LGBTQI+ individuals to proclaim their faith.

As you read each day's scripture and reflection, pray the Holy Spirit breathes revelation deep into your heart, mind, and soul. Pray also that you are open to receiving the message of love he would have you hear.

Above all, remember we are called to this:

Always be ready to give an explanation to anyone who asks you for a reason for your hope, but do it with gentleness and reverence, keeping your conscience clear, so that, when you are maligned, those who defame your good conduct in Christ may themselves be put to shame. For it is better to suffer for doing good, if that be the will of God, than for doing evil.

(1 Peter 3:15-17 NABRE)

May this book equip you to explain your hope.

GUIDE TO TRANSLATIONS

Objections to the legitimacy of LGBTQI+ individuals as Christians are found in widely ranging denominations and traditions. This devotional therefore includes a variety of Bible translations to reflect that diversity. Acronyms for included versions are listed below.

ASV	American Standard Version
ESV	English Standard Version
ISV	International Standard Version
KJV	King James Version
NAB	New American Bible
NABRE	New American Bible Revised Edition
NASB	New American Standard Bible
NIV	New International Version
NKJV	New King James Version
NRSV	New Revised Standard Version
NRSVCE	New Revised Standard Version Catholic Edition
RSV	Revised Standard Version

WHO IS GOD?

Before we begin exploring the scriptural view of the LGBTQI+ community we must first understand the one who breathed life into the collection of books which make up the Bible. Who is this God we worship?

This section is critical because all that follows hinges on who we know God to be. Jesus tells us when we see him, we see the Father. Jesus is the full revelation of God. That means understanding scripture, relationships, and the world around us all hinge on this central question. Who is God?

DAY 1: LOVE

Everyone who loves has been born of God and knows God. Whoever does not love does not know God, because God is love.
(1 John 4: 7-8, NIV)

As you read through scripture, you can find God described as merciful, jealous, compassionate, angry, and forgiving. These adjectives describe God's attributes and responses. But they don't say who God *is*. John's statement above stands out from all the other descriptors in a very powerful way, because it doesn't describe a characteristic or emotion. It proclaims God's very being.

John doesn't say "God is *loving*." He says "God *is* love." That's a world of difference.

Remember the author of the passage is the beloved disciple. The one who reclined at Jesus' side and laid his head on Jesus' shoulder at that final supper. The only male who stood beneath the cross as Jesus suffered and died. The one to whom Jesus entrusted the care of his mother. It can be argued that of all the apostles, John knew Jesus best.

Let's look at John's wonderful proclamation again: "Everyone who loves has been born of God and knows God."

What a powerfully inclusive statement.

A famous hymn written by James Quinn called *Here in Christ we Gather* contains the following refrain:

"God is love, and where true love is
God himself is there."

The name for this devotional came from these lyrics. We are formed in the image and likeness of our creator, and we are called to love. True love is not selfish or judgmental. It is not focused on sex acts. It crosses all genders, races, physical and emotional handicaps, sexual orientations, and other artificial labels designed to create separation between humans. True love springs from God and unites us all into oneness with the beautiful image and likeness of Christ.

Where true love is, God himself is there.

Deep within my existence something said, without any words, "This is what life is supposed to be. You were created to feel deeply and love deeply, without doubt, without shame, and without guilt."

Tim Rymel

DAY 2: FATHER AND GIVER OF GOOD GIFTS

Is there anyone among you who, if your child asks for bread, will give a stone? Or if the child asks for a fish, will give a snake? If you then, who are evil, know how to give good gifts to your children, how much more will your Father in heaven give good things to those who ask him!
(Matthew 7:9-11 NRSV)

In this small segment near the end of Jesus' long set of instructions delivered from a mountaintop, we get a glimpse of the generosity of God's response to our requests. He reminds us the Holy One in heaven is not some authoritarian, disinterested wrath bearer. Rather, he is *Father*.

The child described in this passage is asking merely for sustenance: bread and fish. But many things are needed for us to be healthy, functioning human beings. Maslow's hierarchy of human needs tells us once we are fed we require safety. And once we are safe we require being loved and belonging. And once we belong, we need to be respected. And only once we have these things do we have any chance of becoming fully the people God designed us to be.

Through Maslow's groundbreaking research, it has become widely understood that humans need much more than just food to survive. Our God, Creator and Father, knows this as well, for he is the master designer of humanity.

Who is God? He is our Father. The one to whom we can turn with our requests for acceptance, for belonging, for safety, and for respect. God is the giver of good gifts.

He died not for men, but for each man. If each man had been the only man made, He would have done no less.
C.S. Lewis

4

DAY 3: LIGHT OF THE WORLD

When Jesus spoke again to the people, he said, "I am the light of the world. Whoever follows me will never walk in darkness, but will have the light of life." The Pharisees challenged him, "Here you are, appearing as your own witness; your testimony is not valid." Jesus answered, "Even if I testify on my own behalf, my testimony is valid, for I know where I came from and where I am going. But you have no idea where I come from or where I am going. You judge by human standards; I pass judgment on no one. But if I do judge, my decisions are true, because I am not alone. I stand with the Father, who sent me. In your own Law it is written that the testimony of two witnesses is true. I am one who testifies for myself; my other witness is the Father, who sent me." Then they asked him, "Where is your father?" "You do not know me or my Father," Jesus replied. "If you knew me, you would know my Father also." (John 8:12-19 NIV)

The Pharisees in today's passage bring up the process of law in an effort to invalidate Jesus' message. In response, Jesus tells us he is the light of the world. His brightness is very special. It shines to give clarity about how all things should be viewed; spiritual and physical. Jesus points out that the accusing Pharisees are not viewing things according to the light of Christ, but rather by the dimness of human assessment. He concludes by saying when we know *him*, we know the Father as well. This message was infuriating to those listening.

Jesus chastises the religious elites for not knowing the Father despite their knowledge of the scriptures and their certainty of righteousness. The Pharisees could not align their understanding of God with the man who stood before them with all his radically inclusive, rule-breaking love.

Let's not be like that. Let's recognize that loving acceptance, mercy, and forgiveness *is* in fact Jesus. And let's recognize that when we see Jesus, we see the Father.

The fundamental principle of Christianity is to be what God is, and he is light.
John Hagee

DAY 4: SERVER OF BREAKFAST

After these things Jesus showed himself again to the disciples by the Sea of Tiberias; and he showed himself in this way. Gathered there together were Simon Peter, Thomas called the Twin, Nathanael of Cana in Galilee, the sons of Zebedee, and two others of his disciples. Just after daybreak, Jesus stood on the beach; but the disciples did not know that it was Jesus. Jesus said to them, "Children, you have no fish, have you?" They answered him, "No." He said to them, "Cast the net to the right side of the boat, and you will find some." So they cast it, and now they were not able to haul it in because there were so many fish. That disciple whom Jesus loved said to Peter, "It is the Lord!" When Simon Peter heard that it was the Lord, he put on some clothes, for he was naked, and jumped into the sea. But the other disciples came in the boat, dragging the net full of fish, for they were not far from the land, only about a hundred yards off.

When they had gone ashore, they saw a charcoal fire there, with fish on it, and bread. Jesus said to them, "Bring some of the fish that you have just caught." So Simon Peter went aboard and hauled the net ashore, full of large fish, a hundred fifty-three of them; and though there were so many, the net was not torn. Jesus said to them, "Come and have breakfast."
(John 21:1-2, 4-12 NRSVCE)

Imagine how these followers of Christ felt when they went out to fish after Jesus' crucifixion. They were emotionally drained from the tension of previous days, tired from being awake all night, exhausted by the physical effort of throwing out and pulling in nets, and out of shape because they had been away from this work for so long. They were wet and cold. Going fishing seemed like a logical escape from all the sorrow and fear, but they'd caught nothing.

They were hungry, and the scent of fish cooking must have carried over the water. Jesus stood at the fire the way Peter had while denying Him as the cock crowed. A different rooster crowed this time, at the dawn of this new day. Jesus called for them to bring *more* fish. He wanted the disciples to participate in this feeding. Jesus could have multiplied what he already had. He could have served them cold bread and wine. He could have made manna rain down from the heavens. But he didn't. He made a fire and cooked so the handful of disciples would have warmth and hot food after a cold and lonely night. He tended to their human needs.

Jesus Christ, creator of the universe and all that is in it, cares about our smallest needs. He cares if we are wet and cold. He cares if we are hungry and discouraged. He cares if we are frightened or lonely. He cares if we are marginalized and excluded from Christian fellowship.

John's gospel is the gospel of love, and this story is the one he chose to end it. That positioning shows the immense importance John gave to the story's message. John wanted his last words to us to tell of God's very personal, intimate, and imminent love for us.

Jesus is the yes to every promise of God.
William Barclay

DAY 5: LIKE US IN EVERY RESPECT

*Since, therefore, the children share flesh and blood, he himself likewise
shared the same things, so that through death he might destroy the one who
has the power of death, that is, the devil, and free those who all their lives
were held in slavery by the fear of death. For it is clear that he did not
come to help angels, but the descendants of Abraham. Therefore he had to
become like his brothers and sisters in every respect, so that he might be a
merciful and faithful high priest in the service of God, to make a sacrifice
of atonement for the sins of the people. Because he himself was tested by
what he suffered, he is able to help those who are being tested.*
(Hebrews 2:14-18 NRSV)

Did you catch that? Jesus is like us in *every* respect.

Don't brush this sentence off casually. Let it sink in, deep to the
core of who you are. God is like us in *every* respect. He is like the
transgender woman who is worried she'll be murdered while walking
to her car after work. He is like the broken-hearted gay man who
can't attend the church of his childhood. He is like the bisexual
intersex person who doesn't conform to gender norms and endures
the snide looks and sniggers of strangers. He is like these people just
as much as the heterosexual man who is comfortable performing his
gender in a way this society finds acceptable.

Imagine what it would have been like in the ancient Middle East
to feel gender ambiguity and be afraid to act on it. Imagine the
difficulty of not showing sexual attraction to both genders. Because
he was like us in every respect, he was like each of the people
described above. Jesus' reality was like theirs.

If you are an LGBTQI+ individual, know that Jesus understands
how you feel and cries for your pain. If you are not, remember that
when you offer comfort and aid to one such as this, you offer it to
Christ, himself.

*There is nothing we can do to make God love us more; there is nothing we
can do to make God love us less.*
Philip Yancey

8

DAY 6: OUR JUDGE

For just as the Father has life in himself, so also he gave to his Son the possession of life in himself. And he gave him power to exercise judgment, because he is the Son of Man. Do not be amazed at this, because the hour is coming in which all who are in the tombs will hear his voice and will come out, those who have done good deeds to the resurrection of life, but those who have done wicked deeds to the resurrection of condemnation. Do not think that I will accuse you before the Father: the one who will accuse you is Moses, in whom you have placed your hope.
(John 5:26-29, 45 NABRE)

When discussing LGBTQI+ issues with Christian conservatives we often hear about the God of justice who is ready to bring judgment in the form of fire and eternal torment. But today's passage should give us hope and comfort, regardless of sexual orientation or gender identity. We are all sinners, and the Good News is our judgment will not come from that flame-bearded deity atop an impassable mountain. In today's gospel reading we see *Jesus* will be our judge.

The final line of the passage is a remonstration of the Pharisees for complaining that Jesus healed on the Sabbath. Do you see what Jesus says? He tells them *Moses* will be their accuser because that's where they hold out hope for righteousness. But Jesus tells us the law will not be our accuser unless we set our hope in it.

Christian condemnation of same sex relationships is often based on Old Testament scripture, but many passages prove the law is no longer what it once was. It is no longer the thing we must live by in a vain attempt to be righteous.

As Christians, we have the choice to set our hope in the law or in Him whose mercy triumphs over judgment. Let's set our hope in Him, and pray He will judge us according to our love. And let's pray that Christians who structure so much of their faith around law will have their hearts attuned to the words of Christ.

But all the wickedness in the world that man may do or think is no more to the mercy of God than a live coal dropped in the sea.

William Langford

DAY 7: BEARER OF A HOLY NAME

*Thou shalt not take the name of the Lord thy God in vain; for the Lord will
not hold him guiltless that taketh his name in vain.*
(Exodus 20:7 KJV)

A young woman used the Somali translation of "Jesus Christ" as her Facebook profile name. She is a Christian fundamentalist who picks and chooses scripture to use as whips for LGBTQI+ individuals and others with whom her religiosity disagrees.

A few decades ago, ardent believers wore buttons reading "WWJD?" But given the style with which this girl engages in discussion about homosexuality, it's pretty clear she ignores that essential question.

Because here's what Jesus did:

- He stopped injustice to the marginalized.
- He healed.
- He taught gently, through stories and parables.
- He broke down barriers between those of opposing social positions, cultures, and ideals.
- He excoriated two groups only: the money changers who extorted the faithful, and the scribes and Pharisees who twisted God's instructions and kept people from the love of God.
- He died rather than fight.
- He beseeched God for oneness among his followers.

What he didn't do was use scripture as a cudgel; rather, he proclaimed woe to those who did.

A number of Old Testament passages teach us that Yahweh's name is profaned by hypocritical behavior and false representation of God's words or character. Christians are called to proclaim they come in the name of the Lord. Let's all be careful that when we do so we are truly representing Jesus Christ.

*My idea of God is not a divine idea. It has to be shattered time after time.
He shatters it Himself.*
C.S. Lewis

WHAT IS THE BIBLE? (WEEK ONE)

Last week we examined who God is. We concluded that he is love, he is our Father who gives us good gifts, he is attentive to our every need, and is like us in those needs. We saw that Jesus will be our judge and that we should be careful to act like him if we are to use his name. And we saw that he is the light of the world, by which all things should be understood.

With that understanding, we now look at the Bible. What is it? How are we to view it? For the next two weeks we'll examine texts which help explain how we are to approach the collection of books we call the Bible.

DAY 1: OPENABLE ONLY BY JESUS

I saw a scroll in the right hand of the one who sat on the throne. It had writing on both sides and was sealed with seven seals. Then I saw a mighty angel who proclaimed in a loud voice, "Who is worthy to open the scroll and break its seals?" But no one in heaven or on earth or under the earth was able to open the scroll or to examine it. I shed many tears because no one was found worthy to open the scroll or to examine it. One of the elders said to me, "Do not weep. The lion of the tribe of Judah, the root of David, has triumphed, enabling him to open the scroll with its seven seals." Then I saw standing in the midst of the throne and the four living creatures and the elders a Lamb that seemed to have been slain. He had seven horns and seven eyes; these are the [seven] spirits of God sent out into the whole world. He came and received the scroll from the right hand of the one who sat on the throne. When he took it, the four living creatures and the twenty-four elders fell down before the Lamb. Each of the elders held a harp and gold bowls filled with incense, which are the prayers of the holy ones. They sang a new hymn:

"Worthy are you to receive the scroll and to break open its seals, for you were slain and with your blood you purchased for God those from every tribe and tongue, people and nation." (Revelation 5:1-9 NABRE)

We start our exploration of the scriptures by going to the very end. John's mystical visioning in Revelation reveals the very heart of the issue:

No one in heaven or on earth is able to open the scriptures. We can only peer at the scrolls from behind our various veils and see darkly what is written there. There is only one who is worthy and able, and that is the Lamb of God.

Unless we filter all of our contemplation of the Hebrew and Christian scriptures through the person of Christ, the words are impenetrable. And as our first week's study informed us, the person of Jesus is love. We will revisit this truth throughout the entirety of this book, because it is the key to every argument you face about LGBTQI+ issues.

"No text can be understood out of its entire context. The most 'entire' context is Jesus."

Eugene H. Peterson

DAY 2: CAPABLE OF GIVING WISDOM

But you must continue in the things which you have learned and been assured of, knowing from whom you have learned them, and that from childhood you have known the Holy Scriptures, which are able to make you wise for salvation through faith which is in Christ Jesus. All Scripture is given by inspiration of God, and is profitable for doctrine, for reproof, for correction, for instruction in righteousness, that the man of God may be complete, thoroughly equipped for every good work. (2 Timothy 3:14-17 NKJV)

Paul is held up by many conservative Evangelicals as the supreme authority on who we are to be as Christians. When listening to their positions about LGBTQI+ issues, you might even conclude they hold his statements as more important than those of Jesus himself. In their claims about scripture, a subset of this group talks about The Word of God and the word of God as if they are one and the same. But in taking this position, they defy Paul's instructions to his beloved Timothy. For nowhere does Paul say the Bible and Jesus are essentially the same, and certainly not in today's passage though it is often used in defense of that position.

What Paul says is what we can all agree on: the Holy Scriptures are able to make you wise, though only through faith in Jesus as Paul points out. And the scriptures are profitable, instructive, and useful for equipping us for good work. With these things all Christians can agree.

Next time someone tells you The Word and the word are the same, point them to this passage. Ask them why Paul didn't point the sameness out when writing to the disciple he loved so much, and instructing him on how to lead. Surely this would have been important to know for the man who would become the first Bishop of Ephesus.

Self is the opaque veil that hides the face of God from us. It can be removed only in spiritual experience, never by mere instruction.

A. W. Tozer

DAY 3: INCAPABLE OF PROVIDING ETERNAL LIFE

You search the scriptures, because you think you have eternal life through them; even they testify on my behalf. But you do not want to come to me to have life. (John 5:39-40 NABRE)

Today's passage shows us the more things change, the more they stay the same. The verses come from a discourse Jesus offers after the Jews plot to kill him for breaking the Sabbath and for claiming to be the son of God. He tells them flat out that while they think they can find their salvation through the scriptures, they are wrong.

The religious conservatives of the day knew the scriptures inside and out. They knew the predictions about the messiah and yet when he stood before them, they didn't think he matched their scriptural understanding. They didn't expect him to do things like violate Jewish law, or proclaim Samaritans and Roman pagans had greater faith than they did, or interrupt the righteous stoning of a woman caught in adultery. This was *not* the kind of messiah they anticipated. They wanted the thing they *did* expect; a triumphant king who would kick the Romans out of Jerusalem and be a good and faithful Jew like David. The hyper-religious authorities were so outraged by the Jesus who stood in front of them they decided he had to go. He had to die.

The reason the gospel accounts are important is not merely that they tell us what happened during the days Jesus walked the earth. They are also important because they show us these things are still happening today. Hyper-religious Christians scour the Bible to sculpt a messiah which fits their own ideas of justice, despite the Jesus who sits before them in stories of outrageous, inclusive, love. They proclaim that an inclusive Jesus is fiction, and the real Jesus has eyes of fire and wields a sword of righteous damnation. And like the Jews who demanded the life of Christ, they demand eternal life can only be found through the scriptures and all its accompanying law. Like them, they do not want to come to Jesus to have life. They want to come to the *image* of Jesus they construct from a subset of scriptural passages. The image that matches their view of what he should look and act like.

If Jesus were to walk around with us today, he would undoubtedly be killed again for not matching that image. Like the Jews described in the John 5 passage, too many of us are not willing to look to the radical nature of love as the source for eternal life.

This earth indeed is the very Body of God, and it is from this body that we are born, live, suffer, and resurrect to eternal life. Either all is God's Great Project, or we may rightly wonder whether anything is God's Great Project. One wonders if we humans will be the last to accept this.

Richard Rohr

DAY 4: LIVING AND ACTIVE

For the word of God is living and active and sharper than any two-edged sword. (Hebrews 4:12 NASB)

Evangelical Christians often proclaim the scriptures are alive while simultaneously demanding they are unchanging and unchangeable. But let's look at what it means to have life:

The condition that distinguishes organisms from inorganic objects and dead organisms, being manifested by growth through metabolism, reproduction, and the power of adaptation to environment through changes originating internally.

While this definition applies to organisms, the logic is transferable. If the scriptures are alive, then they can't be unchanging. The only things which don't change are those that are already dead or never contained life in the first place.

The act of living is a process of transformation and change on all sorts of levels. In the case of a plant, water permeates a seed and swells the cells until they burst forth as a shoot and push out into the air. Then air, water, and light are transformed into energy and growth occurs. Eventually flowers come and more seeds are produced and then the plant dies and decomposes and the process of change moves on to some other life form.

The process is similar for pretty much all life: insemination, birth, growth, response to stimuli, death. Only dead things don't grow and adapt to the environment. Dead things merely rot.

So listen up, conservative Evangelical Christians: you have to choose. Either the scriptures are unchanging and therefore dead, or they are living and therefore equipped for change and adaptation, through the power of the Holy Spirit.

To substitute Scripture for the self-revealing Spirit is to put the dead letter in the place of the living Word.
Sebastian Franck

17

DAY 5: SAFELY DEBATABLE

On a Sabbath Jesus was teaching in one of the synagogues
(Luke 13:10 NIV)

Many Christians believe the scriptures are straightforward and their meaning is obvious. They take a literalist approach, claiming the words mean exactly what they say, and that seeking deeper messages is an attempt at manipulation.

Unfortunately for them, the idea is both counter-scriptural and counter-historical. The Jewish tradition of men gathering to debate about the scriptures is thousands of years old. The existence of the Talmud, a collection of writings about those texts, illustrates that interpretation is not straightforward. If it was, why would you need a book of explanations? More recent examples of similar treatises also exist, such as the Roman Catholic Catechism and the Westminster Confession of Faith. We *still* seek tools for exploring the scriptures.

In today's passage, Jesus proves this lack of clarity by teaching about the Hebrew holy books in the synagogue. This is something he does regularly in the gospels. But if the meaning of the scrolls was as straightforward as modern fundamentalists claim, why would he need to explain them?

The people gathered in the synagogue were lucky. Listeners who heard Jesus' explanation of the law and the prophets, of the poetry, allegory, and history, were blessed. They are the only ones who can truly know the scriptures' intended meaning, because they were translated and interpreted by God himself.

Believers since then and until now can only read, study, and pray for the revelation of Christ. We must ask him to speak scriptural mysteries to our hearts just as he did to the listeners in the synagogue. And we can safely argue various points with our fellow believers, just as the faithful have done for millennia.

May Jesus always be the filter through which we interpret the Bible. May we never fear wrestling with its meaning.

One of the few things in life that cannot possibly do harm in the end is the honest pursuit of the truth.
Peter Kreeft

DAY 6: A COLLECTION OF VARYINGLY IMPORTANT PASSAGES

Blessed is the one who keeps the words of the prophecy of this book.
(Revelation 22:7 ESV)

Revelation is one of the trippiest, most difficult, and perhaps even incomprehensible books of the Bible. How can we possibly keep the words of all the prophecy contained within it when we don't have a clue what it means?

Many conservative Christians claim all scripture has equal value for our salvation. The reality is we must apply varying weights and values to different passages and even entire books. How many of us turn to the genealogy listings for comfort or guidance? How many turn to the census data included in Numbers? Are pages full of names as useful to us as the parables Jesus unfolded? Do they help us govern our passions the way Paul counsels in the epistles? Do they offer insight into the passionate love God holds for us the way Solomon professes in his Song of Songs?

It's perfectly okay to acknowledge that some passages are more important than others in the scriptures. If it weren't so, why would we need Jesus' words printed in red as is common in many Bibles? We can believe in the God-breathed nature and inerrancy of the scriptures and still consider some books to be more insightful to the person of Christ and to God himself. We need not demand that every sentence be equally important. We don't have to expect to understand every troubling vision experienced by John or Daniel, and try to "keep" it. It's just not possible.

What we *must* do is hold on to the revelation of the person of Christ; the One who is the way, the truth, and the life. And that way, that truth, and that life, is love.

The death penalty is "biblical" in the same way that war, slavery, and the oppression of women are "biblical." Biblical, but not like Jesus.
Nathan Hamm

DAY 7: THE REVELATION OF GOD'S CHANGING WILL

*About eight days after he said this, he took Peter, John, and James and
went up the mountain to pray. While he was praying his face changed in
appearance and his clothing became dazzling white. And behold, two men
were conversing with him, Moses and Elijah, who appeared in glory and
spoke of his exodus that he was going to accomplish in Jerusalem. Peter
and his companions had been overcome by sleep, but becoming fully awake,
they saw his glory and the two men standing with him. As they were about
to part from him, Peter said to Jesus, "Master, it is good that we are here;
let us make three tents, one for you, one for Moses, and one for Elijah."
But he did not know what he was saying. While he was still speaking, a
cloud came and cast a shadow over them, and they became frightened when
they entered the cloud. Then from the cloud came a voice that said, "This is
my chosen Son; listen to him."*
(Luke 9:28-35 NABRE)

This story comes shortly after Jesus asks the disciples who they think
he is. He listens to their responses but doesn't offer his own
explanation. He leaves that to the Father, who speaks to Peter, John,
and James, about who Christ is. But those three weren't the only ones
being told the news. Notice who else was on the spot for the
revelation: Moses who represents the Law, and Elijah who represents
the Prophets. This is significant.

The two faith heroes are talking with Jesus, and the Father decides
to interrupt their conversation. What might they have been saying?
Were they trying to convince Jesus to follow the old ways?

Peter, James, and John jolt awake to watch in wonder at what is
going on. With typical impetuosity, Peter offers to build tents to
shelter and honor the three of them. His words make Jesus the
equivalent of Elijah and Moses. He says he will build three dwellings:
one for the law, one for the prophets, and one for this newcomer,
Jesus. Three monuments to three institutions.

But the Father breaks in to tell the authors of the Old Testament
something new had come. He doesn't tell Peter, John, and James to

listen to "them." He tells all five of them to listen to Jesus. Even Moses and Elijah. He clarifies there is to be only one tent, one perpetual tabernacle.

The Father made Jesus shine bright on that mountain, outshining those paragons of the Jewish faith. His words made the message even clearer.

The Father says "This is my chosen Son; listen to *him*." May we do so as well.

Preach the Gospel at all times. When necessary, use words.
Commonly attributed to St. Francis of Assisi

WHAT IS THE BIBLE? (WEEK TWO)

Last week our contemplation showed us that:

- Scripture is living and active.
- The scriptures can provide wisdom but cannot give us eternal life.
- Not all verses have the same importance for our salvation.
- It's okay to debate scripture.
- The words of Jesus carry more weight than those of Moses or the Prophets.
- The Bible can only be properly understood when filtered through the words, methods, and actions of Jesus Christ.

This week we look at issues like context, inerrancy, and inspiration. We will encounter examples of contradiction which many fundamentalist-leaning Christians claim don't exist, not for the purpose of proving the Bible wrong, but for discussing what the Bible is truly supposed to be.

The Holy Spirit whispered the messages of the Bible to the writers who captured them. But the Bible is not God. Our Creator wants us to worship him alone, and the Trinity can never be constrained to a box the size of a book on your bedside table.

The contents of this section might seem to fly in the face of what you've been told. Start each contemplation with a prayer that Jesus opens your heart and mind to his truth alone, and to close everything else out. And as you read, remember the words of Jesus: do not be afraid.

Evaluating your understanding of the nature of scripture does not threaten the reality of God, or your relationship with him. If it does, you are worshipping the Bible rather than Jesus Christ.

Fix reason firmly in her seat, and call to her tribunal every fact, every opinion. Question with boldness even the existence of a God; because, if there be one, he must more approve of the homage of reason, than that of blindfolded fear.

Thomas Jefferson

DAY 1: CONTRADICTORY:
TWO CREATION ACCOUNTS

This is the account of the heavens and the earth when they were created,
when the Lord God made the earth and the heavens. Now no shrub had
yet appeared on the earth and no plant had yet sprung up, for the Lord
God had not sent rain on the earth and there was no one to work the
ground, but streams came up from the earth and watered the whole surface
of the ground. Then the Lord God formed a man from the dust of the
ground and breathed into his nostrils the breath of life, and the man
became a living being. (Genesis 2:4-7 NIV)

Then God said, "Let the land produce vegetation: seed-bearing plants and
trees on the land that bear fruit with seed in it, according to their various
kinds." And it was so. The land produced vegetation: plants bearing seed
according to their kinds and trees bearing fruit with seed in it according to
their kinds. And God saw that it was good. And there was evening, and
there was morning—the third day.
(Genesis 1:11-13 NIV)

You will hear there is no contradiction in scripture, but we discover it right in the first chapters of the first book. Two creation accounts are offered, each with a slightly different focus. Chapter 1 gives us the sweeping glory of how the universe came into being, through the mighty bang of God. Chapter 2 focuses more on the advent of mankind. But the descriptions of when humans were created disagree.

In chapter 1 of Genesis, mankind was the *last* thing to be created, after everything else had been put in place. In this account, God made the animals and then humans on the sixth day, and he judged us to be very good. After that, he rested, and admired us; the work of his imagination. So chapter 1's account tells us very clearly plants came into being on the second day. But the passage from chapter 2 above clearly says no shrubs or plants had been created when God formed Adam from the dust.

Which is it? Did God make our planet home filled with greenery on day two, or on day six?

The reality is that it doesn't matter. Genesis was not intended to offer a scientific explanation for how non-being was transformed into being, how nothingness exploded into galaxies. The point is to tell us God was in charge, he had us in mind from the start, and we are to value the great gift of his amazing creation, and of each other.

In these first, conflicting tales, appearing at a place in the Bible which can be no earlier, we are shown the scriptures conflict. But that's okay.

Logically, taking Scripture seriously means being passionately concerned about interpreting it correctly and thus welcoming any evidence that exposes erroneous understandings of the biblical text. Unfortunately, many zealous Bible students and teachers confuse their favorite interpretations of the Bible with the Bible itself.

Hugh Ross

DAY 2: CONTRADICTORY:
THE PUZZLE OF CAIN

*Cain said to the Lord, "My punishment is greater than I can bear! Today
you have driven me away from the soil, and I shall be hidden from your
face; I shall be a fugitive and a wanderer on the earth, and anyone who
meets me may kill me." Then the Lord said to him, "Not so! Whoever
kills Cain will suffer a sevenfold vengeance." And the Lord put a mark
on Cain, so that no one who came upon him would kill him. Then Cain
went away from the presence of the Lord, and settled in the land of Nod,
east of Eden. Cain knew his wife, and she conceived and bore Enoch; and
he built a city, and named it Enoch after his son Enoch.*
(Genesis 4:13-17 NRSV)

Today we return to the story of our initial family, as passed down for
thousands of years by oral tradition until Moses captured it in writing.
Like the creation accounts which offer directly opposing details, this
story illustrates how we must interpret and filter various sections of
the Bible to understand the intent, rather than demanding each line
stand alone as an inarguable truth.

Here we have Cain; the first person to be born of woman. After
killing his brother, Cain was the sole member of his generation, cast
out to wander the earth and find a wife. This presents a few
problems. We have no biblical account of other people having been
directly created by God, and the prevailing Christian understanding is
we are all descendants of Adam and Eve. This means either a) God
did create other people in other lands, and some people therefore did
not descend from Adam and Eve's line, or b) Eve's offspring
described in Genesis 5 had gone into other lands and Cain chose one
of his sisters for a wife, which contradicts laws prohibiting incest.
Some conservative apologists claim it was the latter, and that laws
against incest didn't exist yet so marrying a sister was okay.

We won't try to solve this puzzle here, and shouldn't try, because
the point of these early stories wasn't to explain how the population
of the world occurred scientifically or on a case by case basis. Instead,
this story illustrates how our broken humanity presented itself very
early on. It also illustrates God's mercy by placing on Cain the

protective mark, despite the extremity of his sin. Christ in action, already.

This is key to the interpretation of scripture. We must filter everything, every sentence and story, through the person of Christ.

If we truly knew all the answers in advance as to the meaning of life and the nature of God and the destiny of our souls, our belief would not be a leap of faith and it would not be a courageous act of humanity; it would just be... a prudent insurance policy.

Elizabeth Gilbert

DAY 3: CONTRADICTORY: WAS IT GOD OR SATAN?

Again the anger of the Lord burned against Israel, and he incited David against them, saying, "Go and take a census of Israel and Judah." So the king said to Joab and the army commanders with him, "Go throughout the tribes of Israel from Dan to Beersheba and enroll the fighting men, so that I may know how many there are." But Joab replied to the king, "May the Lord your God multiply the troops a hundred times over, and may the eyes of my lord the king see it. But why does my lord the king want to do such a thing?" (2 Samuel 24:1-3 NIV)

Satan rose up against Israel and incited David to take a census of Israel. So David said to Joab and the commanders of the troops, "Go and count the Israelites from Beersheba to Dan. Then report back to me so that I may know how many there are." But Joab replied, "May the Lord multiply his troops a hundred times over. My lord the king, are they not all my lord's subjects? Why does my lord want to do this? Why should he bring guilt on Israel?" (1 Chronicles 21:1-3 NIV)

1 and 2 Chronicles and 1 and 2 Samuel are a bit like the synoptic gospels in that they contain many of the same stories. They are historic narratives about the first kings of Israel and other events.

The passages above recount the same event; David's call for a census which in the end displeases God and results in Israel being punished with a plague. Both passages open the chapters in which they appear. Both are broken into three verses. Both contain many of the same phrases, and all of the same concepts. With one exception, and that's a doozy.

In the 2 Samuel version, God himself incites David, while in 1 Chronicles it is Satan. Now by any definition, this is a pretty significant difference. The two beings cannot be confused.

A variety of explanations have been offered for these diametrically opposed attributions, but that's not the point for today. The point is if someone tries to tell you scripture doesn't contradict itself, offer these passages. Explaining away the contradictions doesn't make them disappear.

They exist.

The majority of the Bible was written by a minority people living under the rule and reign of massive, mighty empires, from the Egyptian Empire to the Babylonian Empire to the Persian Empire to the Assyrian Empire to the Roman Empire. This can make the Bible a very difficult book to understand if you are reading it as a citizen of the most powerful empire the world has ever seen. Without careful study and reflection, and humility, it may even be possible to miss central themes of the Scriptures.

Rob Bell

DAY 4: CONTRADICTORY:
ON THE FLIGHT TO EGYPT

Now when they had departed, behold, an angel of the Lord appeared to Joseph in a dream and said, "Rise, take the child and his mother, and flee to Egypt, and remain there until I tell you, for Herod is about to search for the child, to destroy him." And he rose and took the child and his mother by night and departed to Egypt. (Matthew 2:13-14 ESV)

And the shepherds returned, glorifying and praising God for all they had heard and seen, as it had been told them. And at the end of eight days, when he was circumcised, he was called Jesus, the name given by the angel before he was conceived in the womb. And when the time came for their purification according to the Law of Moses, they brought him up to Jerusalem to present him to the Lord (as it is written in the Law of the Lord, "Every male who first opens the womb shall be called holy to the Lord") and to offer a sacrifice according to what is said in the Law of the Lord, "a pair of turtledoves, or two young pigeons."
(Luke 2:20-24 ESV)

The narratives offered by Luke and Matthew contradict. Luke offers no mention of Egypt, which in itself is not a problem because not all gospels offer descriptions of the same set of events. The problem comes with the timing of what occurred. Luke describes the shepherds who visited the baby and then moves on to Jesus' circumcision and Mary's purification. Matthew includes the adventures of the three wise men, and the angel's instruction to Joseph to take the family to Egypt to avoid Herod's order to kill all the infants in the region.

And that's where the contradiction comes in. Leviticus 12:1-8 demands women go to the temple in Jerusalem in order to purify their cleanliness after childbirth, and Luke describes the wonderful thing which happened when the priest who served that day encountered the holy family. But Matthew has the three in Egypt, awaiting the death of Herod.

Some biblical apologists find ways to maneuver these details into somehow working. They claim there is time for a return from Egypt before the days of waiting for purification elapse, or the three wise men didn't go to Bethlehem but found them elsewhere, or a variety of other logic maneuvers to assure us these passages don't conflict.

But if we are to take the Bible at face value, because it means what it means what it means, as many conservative Christians demand, then we have a real problem with putting the two narratives of Jesus' infancy together.

What really happened? We don't know. And that's okay. What we do know from these stories is Jesus was believed to be a threat to the political authority and was in danger because of that, right from the beginning. And we know Joseph and Mary were vigilant in following the Jewish law in regard to devotion of firstborn males to God, which allowed them to hear the lovely song of Simeon as he proclaimed the consolation of Israel had finally come.

The Bible contradicts itself. Numerous times. But we take comfort in the One who is our consolation, and *that's* what's important.

To argue with a man who has renounced the use and authority of reason, and whose philosophy consists in holding humanity in contempt, is like administering medicine to the dead, or endeavoring to convert an atheist by scripture.

Thomas Paine

DAY 5: CONTRADICTORY:
PAUL'S DAMASCUS ENCOUNTER

Now as he was going along and approaching Damascus, suddenly a light from heaven flashed around him. He fell to the ground and heard a voice saying to him, "Saul, Saul, why do you persecute me?" He asked, "Who are you, Lord?" The reply came, "I am Jesus, whom you are persecuting. But get up and enter the city, and you will be told what you are to do." The men who were traveling with him stood speechless because they heard the voice but saw no one. (Acts 9:3-7 NRSV)

"While I was on my way and approaching Damascus, about noon a great light from heaven suddenly shone about me. I fell to the ground and heard a voice saying to me, 'Saul, Saul, why are you persecuting me?' I answered, 'Who are you, Lord?' Then he said to me, 'I am Jesus of Nazareth whom you are persecuting.' Now those who were with me saw the light but did not hear the voice of the one who was speaking to me."
(Acts 22:6-9 NRSV)

Today we focus again on contradictions in the Bible. In this case the variances take place within the same book. The first is the account of Paul being knocked off his horse by the voice of Jesus. The second is Paul's proclaiming the story to a group of righteous Jews who believe he preaches blasphemy.

Notice where they differ. They both describe the central action the same way. In Acts 9, the men who were with Paul heard Jesus' voice but did not see the light which blinded him. In Acts 22 however, Paul reports the men who were with him saw the light but didn't hear the voice of God.

These are very significant differences. In one version, the men merely saw the light, which would have been life-changing, though luckily in their case not blinding. They would have had to rely on Paul to tell them what else occurred while that light blazed. In the other version, the men were able to listen to Jesus' proclamations to Paul, and to take to heart his sorrow at the persecution they themselves were participating in.

As we've seen over the past few days, the Bible contradicts itself. But there's no need to be alarmed, because it isn't intended to be used as a technical instruction manual. It's intended to tell the story of our relationship with God throughout history, and to lead up to the wonderful compassion, mercy, and all-encompassing love of Christ.

It is important to learn to understand in a historical text, a text from the past, the living Word of God, that is, to enter into prayer and thus read Sacred Scripture as a conversation with God.

Pope Benedict XVI

DAY 6: WRITTEN BY ERRANT PEOPLE

But to the rest I, not the Lord, say: If any brother has a wife who does not believe, and she is willing to live with him, let him not divorce her.
(1 Corinthians 7:12 NKJV)

Now concerning virgins: I have no commandment from the Lord; yet I give judgment as one whom the Lord in His mercy has made trustworthy.
(1 Corinthians 7:25 NKJV)

What I speak, I speak not according to the Lord, but as it were, foolishly, in this confidence of boasting. (2 Corinthians 11:17 NKJV)

The doctrine of inerrancy is one of the weapons fundamentalist-leaning Christians uses against LGBTQI+ people. Here's how a Roman Catholic document describes it:

Since, therefore, all that the inspired authors, or sacred writers, affirm should be regarded as affirmed by the Holy Spirit, we must acknowledge that the books of Scripture firmly, faithfully and without error teach that truth which God, for the sake of our salvation, wished to see confided to the sacred Scriptures.

Some Christians believe inerrancy applies only to the original manuscripts, while others contend it has been passed along through all the duplications, replications, and translations. Others demand inerrancy only exists in the King James Version. It's an interesting argument, but not one we will take on here.

Look at Paul's words in the passages from the two letters to the Corinthians. In each of these verses, Paul makes it clear he is writing his *own* thoughts, not God's. This introduces a significant logic challenge. If every word in the Bible is inerrant, then what he says *must* be true and therefore the words do not come from God. But if all scripture is God breathed and therefore comes from God, then Paul's words are a lie.

Which is it?

Paul writes to the new Christians in Corinth who have found themselves fractured between teachers who demand different sets of rules be followed. You can almost hear him sighing as he writes, frustrated at the state they are in and their lack of teeth for chewing spiritual meat. He pours out milk in the form of verbal slaps, periodically sweetened with a sprinkle of encouragement. He undoubtedly strove to write what was true and passed along what he thought the Corinthians needed to hear. But just as some people confuse the Bible with God Himself, some people confuse the inerrancy of scripture with the inerrancy of the individual writers. In chapter 7, Paul is so convinced the end is coming soon that he urges people not to marry. He was wrong about that. He was in error. It's thousands of years later, and we are still waiting for Christ to come again.

Can Paul's words be wrong yet still inerrant? For the purposes he was trying to accomplish at that time, yes. But are they the fullness of truth, for all times, places, and situations? No. The epistles were penned by people who did their best to channel the mind of Christ, to people who they assumed wanted to do the same. But those people were not perfect at either end. They were imperfect people writing to imperfect people about perfect truth. Writing *at* that time, *for* that time, without error.

Millennia later we read Paul's words in chapter 11 about how it is a disgrace for men to have long hair, and for women to pray with their head uncovered. We disregard those passages, considering them to be irrelevant artifacts of a bygone culture. We continue in the same chapter, reading the words of the institution of communion, and see them as beautiful words and timelessly applicable. Both views are true.

The concept of inerrancy is a mystery which we cannot solve here on earth. But key to managing the lack of answers is that Jesus didn't leave us a book; he left us a group of followers which we call church. He didn't feed us a book; he fed us himself. He never demanded rigid adherence to a book; he reproved those who did.

We can believe in the God-breathed truth of the scriptures without insisting each line be applied literally to our lives today. And most assuredly, Jesus does not want the idea of inerrancy to be used as a weapon against our fellow brothers and sisters in Christ.

There's a lovely Hasidic story of a rabbi who always told his people that if they studied the Torah, it would put Scripture on their hearts. One of them asked, "Why on our hearts, and not in them?" The rabbi answered, "Only God can put Scripture inside. But reading sacred text can put it on your heart, and then when your hearts break, the holy words will fall inside."

Anne Lamott

DAY 7: ICON NOT IDOL

Thou shalt not make unto thee a graven image, nor any likeness of any thing that is in heaven above, or that is in the earth beneath, or that is in the water under the earth (Exodus 20:4 ASV)

Icons are an ancient form of artwork designed to be windows into heaven via prayer. They aren't meant to be so much looked *at* as *through* to behold the glorious mysteries of God. This is what the Bible should be, but often isn't. Instead, a good number of fundamentalist-leaning Christians conflate Jesus and the Bible. The premise is theoretically based on the opening sentence in John's gospel:

In the beginning was the Word, and the Word was with God, and the Word was God. (John 1:1 ASV)

But there's an impassable chasm of difference between the Word who is God himself, and the Good Word. The very last sentence of John's gospel makes this reality clear:

And there are also many other things which Jesus did, the which if they should be written every one, I suppose that even the world itself would not contain the books that should be written. (John 21:25 ASV)

John tells us just the things Jesus *did* would fill so many books the world could not contain them. And that's just his actions! Actions offer just one avenue of insight into the reality of a being. Through them we can see much, but not the whole. And our God is Triune; three persons, one God. So through the God-breathed, inerrant words of John we know a world filled with books could not describe what Jesus did. This means there is no possible way a single volume we call the Bible can be the same as God himself.

It's simply not possible.

Nowhere in scripture does it say Jesus *is* the Bible. He is THE WORD, and the Bible is his inspired word. But those two are not the same things. We must be very careful not to believe the two are one, because doing so turns the Bible into an idol.

The scriptures should be an icon of God; a window through which we can enter into his mystical reality. But by no means should we turn the Bible into a graven image.

"Concepts create idols; only wonder comprehends anything. People kill one another over idols. Wonder makes us fall to our knees."
Gregory of Nyssa

JESUS AND THE LAW

Many Christians are quick to point out the ways they believe LGBTQI+ individuals violate scriptural injunctions. But it turns out the law is a tricky thing, which the words and actions of Jesus make clear. Over the next three weeks we look at scriptures in which Jesus informs us about how Christians should view Biblical law.

In doing so we discover that Jesus frequently broke Jewish law, that Old Testament law was problematic in many ways, and that love is the fulfillment of the law.

JESUS AS LAWBREAKER

When fundamentalist-leaning Christians use scripture to demand that LGBTQI+ people can't be followers of Jesus, they point to a few Old Testament laws as proof. These arguments are usually coupled with Jesus' words about fulfilling the law, and how not a jot or tittle will change.

What they tend to ignore is the biblical proof that Jesus regularly violated Jewish law in service of the good. This week we explore examples of these violations to help put the law in proper context.

DAY 1: GOD BROKE THE LAW BY BEGETTING JESUS

If within the city a man comes upon a maiden who is betrothed, and has
relations with her, you shall bring them both out to the gate of the city and
there stone them to death: the girl because she did not cry out for help
though she was in the city, and the man because he violated his neighbor's
wife. Thus shall you purge the evil from your midst.
(Deuteronomy 22:23-24 NAB)

Prepare to be shocked.

According to today's Deuteronomy passage, God himself violated the law by the very begetting of Jesus.

Luke chapter 1 describes the occurrence. Mary was within a city; the town of Nazareth. She was betrothed to Joseph. The Holy Spirit came upon her, overshadowed her, and planted a child in her womb. She did not cry out for help because she didn't want or need it. As proof this was an infraction, Joseph believed he'd been wronged and planned to divorce her.

All of these facts line up to show a clear violation of the law laid out in Deuteronomy 22.

So at the very moment the new covenant was initiated, God himself broke an old covenant law related to sex and marriage. It was a sign of its passing, a tearing of a holy scroll which was worshiped by the religious right of the day.

The Spirit must have whispered to Mary "Don't think about what you've been taught. Simply love me with all your heart and with all your soul and with all your strength." Mary responded by opening to his request, despite knowing she could be stoned to death as a result.

Since God begins the very life of Christ through a violation of marital law, it certainly points out that his followers' view of law needed to change, and drastically.

What if Jesus was not offering his followers an ethical system to follow, but
rather was inviting them to enter into a life of love that transcends ethics, a
life of liberty that dwells beyond religious laws? The difference between

following an ethical system and being consumed by love can be seen in the way that ethical systems seek to provide a way to work out what needs to be done so that it can be carried out. In contrast, love is never constrained, it never sits back, it always seeks to do more than what is demanded of it.

Peter Rollins

DAY 2: JESUS BROKE THE SABBATH REPEATEDLY

And this was why the Jews were persecuting Jesus, because he was doing these things on the Sabbath. But Jesus answered them, "My Father is working until now, and I am working." This was why the Jews were seeking all the more to kill him, because not only was he breaking the Sabbath, but he was even calling God his own Father, making himself equal with God. (John 5:16-18 ESV)

When trying to wrap your head around the idea that being an LGBTQI+ Christian is okay, it's important to remember something extremely significant: Jesus himself broke the law. Numerous times.

Most conservative and evangelical Christians will argue with you about this. They'll first tell you it never happened, and then when you offer examples they'll explain it away, trying to say he was just going against either the hypocrisy of the Pharisees or the rules they made up. But today's passage is proof their claims are scripturally wrong.

The Sabbath was so important in the Old Testament that it's even included in the Ten Commandments. Rules relating to it are outlined in Leviticus, Deuteronomy, Numbers, and other books. Numbers 15:32-36 tells the story of a man who collected firewood on the Sabbath being taken out of the camp and stoned to death as punishment. Clearly, violating the rules for inactivity on the Lord's Day was a big deal.

Then here comes Jesus, who breaks those rules repeatedly. In today's passage we see that the Jews were ready to dole out the punishment required by law for his insolence.

The other argument you'll hear is that the law was made for humans rather than for God, which is, of course, true. But that doesn't change the reality of Jesus' actions which were intentional violations.

Jesus broke the law. Indisputably. For his own reasons: to establish a new order for those of us in the kingdom who still walk around on the earth, and to show us love is more important than law.

It is no coincidence that Christian fundamentalist movements worldwide seek a return to Old Testament laws - because they fundamentally reject Christ as the New Covenant - which replaced all that. They are not Christians—they are Leviticans.

Christina Engela

DAY 3: JESUS DEFENDS BREAKING THE SABBATH

*As he was passing through a field of grain on the sabbath, his disciples
began to make a path while picking the heads of grain. At this the
Pharisees said to him, "Look, why are they doing what is unlawful on the
sabbath?" He said to them, "Have you never read what David did when
he was in need and he and his companions were hungry? How he went into
the house of God when Abiathar was high priest and ate the bread of
offering that only the priests could lawfully eat, and shared it with his
companions?" Then he said to them, "The sabbath was made for man, not
man for the sabbath." (Mark 2:23-27 NABRE)*

Man was not made for the Sabbath. Unlike men, the Sabbath isn't a
thing which must be fed. It was created so humans would take a day
away from the grinding demands of life in order to focus on God,
because we so desperately need that periodic focus. God created it
knowing our minds and hearts so easily turn away from the reality of
his love, light, and justice to look at the darkness which surrounds us
and tempts us to look at each other and create labels of differentness,
rather than looking at him and his truth.

The Pharisees had a hard time remembering that essential purpose.
Instead of working to ensure the people within their spiritual care
strove to honor God through sacrifices of mercy (Hosea 6:6, Matthew
9:13), they yammered and hammered about jots and tittles.

In this case, Jesus' disciples were hungry. They were traveling
which in itself was a violation of the Sabbath:

*Bear in mind that the LORD has given you the Sabbath; that is why on
the sixth day he gives you bread for two days. Everyone is to stay where
they are on the seventh day; no one is to go out. (Exodus 16:29)*

We don't know where they were headed, or how long it had been
since they'd eaten. Walking builds up an appetite, and Jesus' disciples
were apparently hungry enough to break the law by gathering grain as
they walked.

Most importantly in this story is that Jesus defended them. He
didn't defend the Pharisees or rebuke his friends. He attempted to

adjust the wrong-headedness of the Pharisees' views on what a day dedicated to the Lord was supposed to mean.

Jesus had to walk on the perilous confines of reason and religion: and a step to right or left might place him within the gripe of the priests of the superstition, a blood thirsty race, as cruel and remorseless as the being whom they represented as the family God of Abraham, of Isaac and of Jacob, and the local God of Israel. They were constantly laying snares, too, to entangle him in the web of the law.

Thomas Jefferson

DAY 4: PHARISEES SEEK JESUS' DEATH DUE TO HIS VIOLATIONS

Again he entered the synagogue. There was a man there who had a withered hand. They watched him closely to see if he would cure him on the sabbath so that they might accuse him. He said to the man with the withered hand, "Come up here before us." Then he said to them, "Is it lawful to do good on the sabbath rather than to do evil, to save life rather than to destroy it?" But they remained silent. Looking around at them with anger and grieved at their hardness of heart, he said to the man, "Stretch out your hand." He stretched it out and his hand was restored. The Pharisees went out and immediately took counsel with the Herodians against him to put him to death. (Mark 3:1-6 NABRE)

Today's passage picks up from yesterday's. It's the opening of the third chapter of Mark's good news, while yesterday closed out chapter two. The two are connected, and continue the same theme. Remember; the original documents did not contain chapter breaks and verse numbering. Chapter designations didn't come into use until the 13th century, and verses appeared for the first time in the 16th century. So in Mark's thinking, these two stories were meant to go together.

In today's story of Jesus' lawbreaking ways, he hits the issue head on. What is lawful to do on the Sabbath? Are we to abide by each and every rule Moses laid out, or are we to look at the bigger picture of what God has requested through the person of his Son?

The Pharisees thought it was better to leave people in desperately hurting situations rather than violate the letter of the law. This made Jesus angry. It made him grieve. He offered them the choice: to do good or evil. Their response was to choose evil, immediately plotting with the Herodians to destroy him. Their identities were so pridefully connected to their religious understanding that they wanted to stop his words from ever being spoken again. And Jesus was grieved.

Jesus is still grieving because modern day Pharisees continue to persecute those who don't follow the particular set of laws they demand be followed to the letter. Let's try not to be part of that grief.

> *If Bible-believing Christians are asked how they can justify setting aside great blocks of divine commands in the Old Testament as "truth for today," even the most avowed scriptural literalists among them respond: because we are no longer living under the old covenant but the new.*
> *Exactly!*
> C. S. Cowles

DAY 5: JESUS SUGGESTS VIOLATING A COMMANDMENT

Now when Jesus saw great crowds around him, he gave orders to go over to the other side. A scribe then approached and said, "Teacher, I will follow you wherever you go." And Jesus said to him, "Foxes have holes, and birds of the air have nests; but the Son of Man has nowhere to lay his head." Another of his disciples said to him, "Lord, first let me go and bury my father." But Jesus said to him, "Follow me, and let the dead bury their own dead." (Matthew 8:18-22 NRSVCE)

Here Jesus goes again, breaking the law, or at least, telling his followers to do so.

Burial customs were extremely important, but there don't seem to be many laws regarding them. You can find prohibitions about uncleanliness related to touching the dead, and there are passages about the death and burial of many prominent figures. Deuteronomy 21:23 instructs us to bury a man on the same day he was hanged, but that's about the most specific instruction you'll find.

But we do know it was an obligation for family members to bury their dead, and an act of piety for Jews to bury those outside their families when necessary.

More importantly for this passage however is the commandment to honor our parents. This is one of the biggies. The top ten. The ones overarching all the Levitical laws and instructions which came afterward.

In today's passage, the scribe disciple asked to bury his father. He asked to fulfill his familial obligation to perform a final, ultimate act of honoring. An act which is a significant milestone in each of our lives.

And yet Jesus told him not to.

Of course he had his purposes. Presumably this is Jewish hyperbole in action. But the truth is the truth: Jesus advised his disciple to go against Jewish custom, and to break one of the Ten Commandments. Jesus was a law breaker.

> *The yoke is hard because the teachings of Jesus are radical: enemy love, unconditional forgiveness, extreme generosity. The yoke is easy because it is accessible to all — the studied and the ignorant, the rich and the poor, the religious and the nonreligious. Whether we like it or not, love is available to all people everywhere to be interpreted differently, applied differently, screwed up differently, and manifested differently.*
>
> Rachel Held Evans

DAY 6: JESUS VIOLATES PURIFICATION LAWS

And there was a woman who had had a discharge of blood for twelve years, and who had suffered much under many physicians, and had spent all that she had, and was no better but rather grew worse. She had heard the reports about Jesus and came up behind him in the crowd and touched his garment. For she said, "If I touch even his garments, I will be made well." And immediately the flow of blood dried up, and she felt in her body that she was healed of her disease. And Jesus, perceiving in himself that power had gone out from him, immediately turned about in the crowd and said, "Who touched my garments?" And his disciples said to him, "You see the crowd pressing around you, and yet you say, 'Who touched me?'" And he looked around to see who had done it. But the woman, knowing what had happened to her, came in fear and trembling and fell down before him and told him the whole truth. And he said to her, "Daughter, your faith has made you well; go in peace, and be healed of your disease."
(Mark 5:25-34 ESV)

The brave woman who approached Jesus in this story is a lawbreaker. Instructions for menstruating women listed in Leviticus 15 included isolation so they would not cause others to become ritually impure. She would have been housebound for years because of this unexplained and incurable issue of blood. Her life would have been severely curtailed as she was stuck within the confines of the walls of her home.

But out she goes into the crowd, having heard Jesus was passing through town, and hoping and praying he might heal her. She compounds her "sinfulness" by touching his garment, despite knowing she was defiling him in the process.

It was not her fault that she had been bleeding for years. It was governed by some internal mystery of organs and hormones, and was not fixable despite her efforts to try and change it. The same thing is true for LGBTQI+ people. Their gender and sexual orientation is not something controllable or chosen. It cannot be "fixed" through conversion therapy or stern biblical admonitions. It simply is. These people should not be confined to closets as this woman with the issue of blood had been.

It was not her strict adherence to the rites and rituals of religion that made her whole. It was her faith. And that faith allowed her to go in peace.

Meanwhile, Jesus continued along his way to resurrect the dead daughter of a religious official, despite knowing he'd been made ritually unclean. He did not stop for ritual purification. He went on, in violation of the law, to continue his ministry.

Jesus was consistently on the side of those who were outcast by society and bore the unfair burden of disdain, discrimination, and prejudice. It is likely that he would look at modern-day lesbian, gay, bisexual, and transgender people and hold real sympathy for them and their plight. He would have understood the implications of a system set up to benefit the heterosexual majority over the homosexual minority. It is hard to imagine Jesus joining in the wholesale discrimination against LGBT people. Isn't it logical that he would be sympathetic to young gay teens who take their own lives rather than live with the stigma attached to their sexual orientation? Would he not be found speaking a word of support, encouragement, and hope to them? Would he not be seeking a change in the hearts of those who treat them as outcasts?

The Right Reverend Gene Robinson

DAY 7: JESUS COMMANDS THE CONSUMPTION OF BLOOD

Then Jesus said to them, "Most assuredly, I say to you, unless you eat the flesh of the Son of Man and drink His blood, you have no life in you. Whoever eats My flesh and drinks My blood has eternal life, and I will raise him up at the last day. For My flesh is food indeed, and My blood is drink indeed. He who eats My flesh and drinks My blood abides in Me, and I in him. As the living Father sent Me, and I live because of the Father, so he who feeds on Me will live because of Me. This is the bread which came down from heaven—not as your fathers ate the manna, and are dead. He who eats this bread will live forever." These things He said in the synagogue as He taught in Capernaum.

Therefore many of His disciples, when they heard this, said, "This is a hard saying; who can understand it?" When Jesus knew in Himself that His disciples complained about this, He said to them, "Does this offend you?" (John 6:53-61 NKJV)

In this translation, this section is titled "Many Disciples Turn Away". The disciples must have been terribly scandalized by Jesus words. He knew it, because he asked them if they found the idea offensive. Because they were good Jews, they *were* offended, and here's why:

If anyone of the house of Israel or of the aliens who reside among them eats any blood, I will set my face against that person who eats blood, and will cut that person off from the people. For the life of the flesh is in the blood; and I have given it to you for making atonement for your lives on the altar; for, as life, it is the blood that makes atonement. Therefore I have said to the people of Israel: No person among you shall eat blood, nor shall any alien who resides among you eat blood.
(Leviticus 17:10-12 NRSV)

Jesus knew the scriptures well enough to correct the Pharisees and teach in the temple, yet here he demands something which goes directly against the Law of Moses. Talk about drinking blood would have been shocking and revolting to this group which was raised to keep kosher. Blood was *not* to be consumed. Whether you view communion as mere symbol, as containing the real presence of Jesus,

55

or as a transformation of bread and wine to his body and blood, doesn't really matter in this context. We are talking about the understanding of blood in Jesus' day, and the reaction of his disciples: many of them turned away.

Jesus said these scandalous things within the context of a long-standing, beloved liturgy. Prayers over bread and cup at the Passover meal were well established standards and still are. So Jesus had the audacity to change prayers which had been prayed for generations, and to tell them to drink his very blood.

Both of these things were shocking violations of Jewish law and custom. It's a miracle any of the disciples remained.

If zeal had been appropriate for putting humanity right, why did God the Word clothe himself in the body, using gentleness and humility in order to bring the world back to his Father?

St. Isaac the Syrian

LAW AS PROBLEMATIC

Last week we walked with Jesus as he broke a variety of Jewish laws so we would have a model for our own evaluation of behavior. This week we look at scriptures which describe problems related to the law and Jesus' words related to those problems.

DAY 1: THE LETTER KILLS

Not that we are sufficient of ourselves to think of anything as being from ourselves, but our sufficiency is from God, who also made us sufficient as ministers of the new covenant, not of the letter but of the Spirit; for the letter kills, but the Spirit gives life.
(2 Corinthians 3:5-6 NKJV)

The Pharisees most often mentioned in the gospels are the ones who wielded the law like a scythe to cut down those who didn't follow every jot and tittle. Of course no one *could* obey the letter of the law completely, which is why Christ came; to fulfill it. Our modern day Pharisees still demand such obedience, though they pick and choose which laws are okay to be discarded. Many see it as a noble duty, a supreme calling from God himself, just as Paul no doubt did at the stoning of Stephen in Acts chapter 7.

But look at these glorious words from Paul, whose writing often wavers between his Pharisaical training and the wonderful new freedom of Christ. He tells us our "sufficiency," our "enoughness," doesn't come from straining to follow the letter of the law. It doesn't even say we are to follow the *spirit* of the law. He says our sufficiency, our adequacy, comes from Christ. Not only that; he reports that God equips us to be ministers of the Spirit.

Jesus doesn't make us sufficient so we can be law-wielders, for, Paul tells us the letter *kills*. When we wield the law as the modern day Pharisees do, using it as a weapon, it is a weapon of death. Christians are not supposed to be death wielders. We are called to be ministers of the life-giving Spirit.

The dying thief had, perhaps, disobeyed the will of God in many things: but in the most important event of his life he listened and obeyed. The Pharisees had kept the law to the letter and had spent their lives in the pursuit of a most scrupulous perfection. But they were so intent upon perfection as an abstraction that when God manifested His will and His perfection in a concrete and definite way they had no choice but to reject it.
Thomas Merton

DAY 2: PERFECTION CANNOT BE ACHIEVED THROUGH LAW

If perfection could have been attained through the Levitical priesthood— and indeed the law given to the people established that priesthood—why was there still need for another priest to come, one in the order of Melchizedek, not in the order of Aaron? For when the priesthood is changed, the law must be changed also. He of whom these things are said belonged to a different tribe, and no one from that tribe has ever served at the altar. For it is clear that our Lord descended from Judah, and in regard to that tribe Moses said nothing about priests. The former regulation is set aside because it was weak and useless (for the law made nothing perfect), and a better hope is introduced, by which we draw near to God. And it was not without an oath! Others became priests without any oath, but he became a priest with an oath when God said to him: "The Lord has sworn and will not change his mind: 'You are a priest forever.'" Because of this oath, Jesus has become the guarantor of a better covenant.
(Hebrews 7:11-14, 18-22 NIV)

Conservative Christians vehemently claim the entirety of scripture still applies and remains in place for today's faithful. But the counsel to the Hebrews above offers a very different view of the law.

The first line alone sums it up: If perfection can be attained through the old way of doing things, i.e. by following the letter of the law and going to priests for sacrificial removal of our sins against that law, then why was Jesus needed? Why did we need a priest who goes back to the time before the law existed?

But the priesthood *did* change, and as the passage says, the law must be changed also. The old regulations were set aside as weak, useless, and making nothing perfect.

Jesus is the ultimate law breaker. He became high priest when the Bible is clear priests come from the tribe of Levi, not Judah. In that becoming, he brings a better covenant, a better hope, and a better law through which we draw near to God.

Perfection cannot be achieved through the law. It comes only through Jesus.

You can avoid Jesus as Savior by keeping all the moral laws. If you do that, then you have "rights." God owes you answered prayers, and a good life, and a ticket to heaven when you die. You don't need a Savior who pardons you by free grace, for you are your own Savior.

Timothy J. Keller

DAY 3: JESUS POINTS OUT FLAWS IN THE LAW

Moses told the elders of the Israeli tribes, "This is what the Lord has commanded: 'When a man makes a vow to the Lord, or swears an oath—an obligation that is binding to himself—he is not to break his word. Instead, he is to fulfill whatever promise came out of his mouth.'"
(Numbers 30:1-2 ISV)

The Numbers passage provides instructions about swearing oaths. This translation even uses the phrase "the Lord has commanded," so clearly it was not some trifling rule. Making oaths in God's name was common practice in the day of Moses. But when the time came for the law to be fulfilled through Christ, we were directed not to make oaths at all:

"Again, you have heard that it was said to the people long ago, 'Do not break your oath, but fulfill to the Lord the vows you have made.' But I tell you, do not swear an oath at all: either by heaven, for it is God's throne; or by the earth, for it is his footstool; or by Jerusalem, for it is the city of the Great King. And do not swear by your head, for you cannot make even one hair white or black. All you need to say is simply 'Yes' or 'No'; anything beyond this comes from the evil one."
(Matthew 5:33-37 ISV)

Jesus tells us we are simply to let our word be enough. But he says a lot more than that. Take a look at the last verse in the Matthew passage. Jesus says oaths actually come from the evil one.

Moses told us making vows and swearing oaths is perfectly fine as long as we fulfill them. Jesus contradicts this concept so strongly he actually says vows come from Satan.

Apparently there was a problem with the old law. Otherwise, Jesus would not have turned it so completely on its head.

In the Sermon on the Mount, Jesus said, "You have heard it said…but I say unto you." Jesus took the Old Testament laws to a deeper level of meaning and obedience, from the "letter of the Law" to the "Spirit of the Law." Following the letter of the law was the dead "religion" of which Barth, among others, had written. It was man's attempt to deceive God

into thinking one was being obedient, which was a far greater deception.
God always required something deeper than religious legalism.

Eric Metaxas

DAY 4: THE LAW IS A SHADOW

Now every high priest is appointed to offer gifts and sacrifices; thus the necessity for this one also to have something to offer. They worship in a copy and shadow of the heavenly sanctuary, as Moses was warned when he was about to erect the tabernacle. For he says, "See that you make everything according to the pattern shown you on the mountain." Now he has obtained so much more excellent a ministry as he is mediator of a better covenant, enacted on better promises. For if that first covenant had been faultless, no place would have been sought for a second one.
(Hebrews 8:3, 5-7 NABRE)

Somewhere along the line we have come to think that since scripture is perfect, the Law, which is in scripture, must also be perfect. Because of this, conservative Christians scramble to figure out how the Law still remains completely intact, while simultaneously believing many of its rules no longer apply. This requires rigorous mental gymnastics which inevitably result in exhaustion and abandonment of the question. But the law was not perfect, according to many New Testament scriptures, including today's.

God showed Moses a vision of the traveling tabernacle he was to build, but immediately humanity intervened with all its imperfections. We are simply unable to create anything that exists in heavenly perfection here on earth. It is impossible.

In Jesus, the barriers to perfection are removed. He is the perfect sanctuary in which we can trust. He is the replacement for a flawed covenant. He is fulfillment of the law.

When we read the law, we should not view it as a list of perfect instructions set down for us by God. We should view it as an imperfect construct put into place for a season, and now that season has passed.

People who cling to a legalistic view of God are worshiping in a mere shadow of the true sanctuary. Let's worship Jesus instead.

Jesus lived and died in vain if He did not teach us to regulate the whole of life by the eternal law of love.
Mahatma Gandhi

DAY 5: LAW CREATES UNHOLY ZEAL

Brothers and sisters, my heart's desire and prayer to God for the Israelites is that they may be saved. For I can testify about them that they are zealous for God, but their zeal is not based on knowledge. Since they did not know the righteousness of God and sought to establish their own, they did not submit to God's righteousness. Christ is the culmination of the law so that there may be righteousness for everyone who believes.
(Romans 10:1-4 NIV)

How interesting that Paul prayed for the Israelites to be saved! He knew their zeal first hand, having been among the most zealous of the faithful. They strived so hard to follow the rules and regulations of Jewish law and tradition, fervently believing doing so would earn them entrance into God's kingdom.

But Paul's words contain an interestingly subtle point. He says they would not *submit* to God's righteousness. This connotes pride, because submission requires humility. The zealous often have difficulty in this area. Their zeal (like that of today's conservative Christians) was marked by certainty sprung not from faith in God, but from faith in the correctness of their particular interpretation of scripture. Those ancient Israelites sought a righteousness of their own creation. Moderns do the same.

How do we overcome this susceptibility?

First, seek to *know* God. Studying the scriptures can help, but remember you don't form relationships by reading. Relationship comes from interaction. Pray. Talk to God. Ask for revelation from the Holy Spirit.

Second, seek to know *God* rather than a set of rules. When you look to the scriptures for insight, remember the Father sent the Son as the *fullness of revelation* about his being. Look therefore to Jesus for the most complete scriptural picture.

Third, repeat Paul's final sentence in this passage:

Christ is the culmination of the law so that there may be righteousness for everyone who believes.

Christ is the culmination of the law. Righteousness comes not through slavish obedience to rules, but through belief in him. Rest in this, and pray for our zealous Christian brothers and sisters just as Paul prayed for the zealous Israelites.

You think that your laws correct evil - they only increase it. There is but one way to end evil - by rendering good for evil to all men without distinction.

Leo Tolstoy

DAY 6: LAW IS TOO HEAVY TO CARRY

One of the experts in the law answered him, "Teacher, when you say these things, you insult us also." Jesus replied, "And you experts in the law, woe to you, because you load people down with burdens they can hardly carry, and you yourselves will not lift one finger to help them. "Woe to you, because you build tombs for the prophets, and it was your ancestors who killed them. So you testify that you approve of what your ancestors did; they killed the prophets, and you build their tombs. Because of this, God in his wisdom said, 'I will send them prophets and apostles, some of whom they will kill and others they will persecute.' Therefore this generation will be held responsible for the blood of all the prophets that has been shed since the beginning of the world, from the blood of Abel to the blood of Zechariah, who was killed between the altar and the sanctuary. Yes, I tell you, this generation will be held responsible for it all.
(Luke 11:45-51 NIV)

Oh, the power of that very first sentence!

Jesus, the fulfillment of the Hebrew Scripture's prophecy and law, appears among the religious experts, hoping they will have ears to hear his transformative, radical proclamation of love. In response, they are insulted. How dare a humble carpenter from the insignificant town of Nazareth try to teach them anything about God?

How dare a queer young man living in an ultraconservative small town in the Bible belt? How dare a transgender woman of color? How dare the devout Catholic mother of a daughter who just came out as lesbian?

Those ancient Pharisees and experts in the law approved of the way their ancestors treated the prophets of the day; killing and persecuting them so they wouldn't have to listen to messages of repentance. Today's Pharisees and experts in the law do the same, bragging about their moral superiority in condemning voices of tolerance, acceptance, and love.

LGBTQI+ are persecuted and sometimes even murdered just for trying to live their lives authentically. Those lives can never be restored. There is no comforting the broken hearts of their loved ones. But we know this; the religious experts who contribute to those deaths through hateful rhetoric and rejection will be held responsible for the bloodshed.

Woe be it to them.

Moral courage is a rarer commodity than bravery in battle or great intelligence. Yet it is the one essential, vital quality of those who seek to change a world which yields most painfully to change.

Robert F. Kennedy

Day 7: Law Creates Judgment Based on Appearances

Now at the festival the Jewish leaders were watching for Jesus and asking, "Where is he?" Among the crowds there was widespread whispering about him. Some said, "He is a good man." Others replied, "No, he deceives the people." But no one would say anything publicly about him for fear of the leaders. Not until halfway through the festival did Jesus go up to the temple courts and begin to teach. The Jews there were amazed and asked, "How did this man get such learning without having been taught?" Jesus answered, "My teaching is not my own. It comes from the one who sent me. Anyone who chooses to do the will of God will find out whether my teaching comes from God or whether I speak on my own. Whoever speaks on their own does so to gain personal glory, but he who seeks the glory of the one who sent him is a man of truth; there is nothing false about him. Has not Moses given you the law? Yet not one of you keeps the law. Why are you trying to kill me?"

"You are demon-possessed," the crowd answered. "Who is trying to kill you?"

Jesus said to them, "I did one miracle, and you are all amazed. Yet, because Moses gave you circumcision (though actually it did not come from Moses, but from the patriarchs), you circumcise a boy on the Sabbath. Now if a boy can be circumcised on the Sabbath so that the law of Moses may not be broken, why are you angry with me for healing a man's whole body on the Sabbath? Stop judging by mere appearances, but instead judge correctly." (John 7:11-24 NIV)

You have probably heard it said that Christians who support LGBTQI+ rights are deceivers, and perhaps even demonically afflicted. Maybe those things have been said about you. If so, you are in exceedingly good company. When Jesus broke the law regarding the Sabbath, the religious experts proclaimed both things about him (and worse).

His response was to point out that:

1. *None* of the religious purists kept the whole law. They were therefore in no position to point fingers.

2. Those who earnestly strive to do the will of God and seek to give him glory understand Jesus' radically inclusive love *is* the will of the Father.

3. Judging people through the lens of law rather than through the law of love is equivalent to judging by appearances.

Next time someone hurls accusations at you about being a deceiver, or being demon-influenced, don't bother trying to use logic in response. Simply point them to this passage, and highlight what Jesus had to say.

The moral law may exist to be transcended: but there is no transcending it for those who have not first admitted its claims up on them, and then tried with all their strength to meet that claim, and fairly and squarely faced the fact of their failure.

C.S. Lewis

JESUS AS FULFILLMENT OF THE LAW

In our final week of examining the law, we contemplate how Jesus fulfills it, through his time on earth and on the cross.

DAY 1: JESUS' COMMANDMENTS TRUMP ALL LAW

When the Pharisees heard that he had silenced the Sadducees, they gathered together, and one of them, a lawyer, asked him a question to test him. "Teacher, which commandment in the law is the greatest?" He said to him, "'You shall love the Lord your God with all your heart, and with all your soul, and with all your mind. This is the greatest and first commandment. And a second is like it: 'You shall love your neighbor as yourself.' On these two commandments hang all the law and the prophets."
(Matthew 22:34-40 RSV)

Then one of the scribes came, and having heard them reasoning together, perceiving that He had answered them well, asked Him, "Which is the first commandment of all?" Jesus answered him, "The first of all the commandments is: 'Hear, O Israel, the Lord our God, the Lord is one. And you shall love the Lord your God with all your heart, with all your soul, with all your mind, and with all your strength.' This is the first commandment. And the second, like it, is this: 'You shall love your neighbor as yourself.' There is no other commandment greater than these."
(Mark 12:28-31 NKJV)

Many Bibles print the words of Jesus in red, and with a quick scan we can see how much of the text is made up of his speech. The gospels include a great deal of red ink, much of it instructions for how to get to heaven. Some of these instructions appear to be conflicting, and have led to fierce arguments among Christians which ultimately resulted in denominational splits. But in today's passage we look at the word "commandment."

It is a special word, one which is not used all that much in our scriptures. You will generally find it only in reference to the words stamped on the tablets Moses bore down the mountain, and to verses like today's.

That should make us pay attention. We find Jesus using the phrase "command" and "commandment" rarely, and when he does, it is always in a similar context to the above. It is always a command to love.

"Command" has a very special meaning. It is not the same as to instruct, or urge, or proclaim, or exhort. It stands alone in virtue of its concrete, authoritative, definitive nature. It is very close in meaning to the word "demand."

The Ten Commandments trumped all the other laws and rules developed over time as delivered by Moses or developed by the religious authorities. And the commandments of Jesus override everything which came before.

And so I discovered that it is not on our forgiveness any more than on our goodness that the world's healing hinges, but on His. When He tells us to love our enemies, He gives, along with the command, the love itself.

Corrie ten Boom

DAY 2: THIS IS THE LAW AND THE PROPHETS

Therefore, whatever you want men to do to you, do also to them, for this is the Law and the Prophets. (Matthew 7:12 NKJV)

In several places throughout the gospels Jesus corrects the Jewish understanding of the law. A few times he summarizes those sets of rules as "the Law and the Prophets." This is one example of that summary.

His words have become known as the Golden Rule; a concept taught by Christians and non-Christians alike. We know the idea so well we don't even have to say the whole phrase. We can just say "Do unto others…" and everyone knows what follows.

You might notice the passage begins with the word "therefore." This is because the sentence is a follow-on to his preceding words. The seventh chapter of Matthew opens with Jesus' warning against judging others, and is followed by a reminder that God is the Father who wants to be sought and found, and who gives good gifts. Because of this positioning of thought, we can conclude Jesus meant we are to be generous with our neighbors, both in our judgment of them, and with ourselves.

Do unto others what you would have done unto you.

If you are an LGBTQI+ individual, this means you should treat those who disagree with you with dignity and respect. You should try to enlighten minds darkened through no fault of their own.

And if you are someone who struggles to believe Christianity can include LGBTQI+ individuals, you should seek both to understand what it might be like to live their lives, and to recognize and work toward their civil and human rights.

"God's truth!" one side shouts. "More loving!" comes the response.

But there shouldn't be a clash between 'God's truth' and 'More loving.' In the Bible, Truth and Love are two sides of the same coin. You can't have one without the other. God's Truth is all about God's Love for us and the Love we ought to have for one another. We are being untrue to that Truth if we treat people unlovingly. And we are missing out on the full extent of that Love if we try to divorce it from Ultimate Truth.

Justin Lee

DAY 3: JESUS FULFILLS THE LAW

"Do not think that I have come to abolish the law or the prophets; I have come not to abolish but to fulfill. For truly I tell you, until heaven and earth pass away, not one letter, not one stroke of a letter, will pass from the law until all is accomplished." (Matthew 5:17-18 NRSV)

Today we examine a phrase which modern day Pharisees fling about when lambasting LGBTQI+ individuals for their "lifestyle." They repeat Jesus' words about neither jot nor tittle passing away, and demand the law somehow remains through him, unchanged. To their credit, they earnestly believe that his statement about fulfillment means things are to stay the same. But they skip the critical phrase that follows, which reads "…until all is accomplished."

And guess what? It all *has* been accomplished, at least according to John.

John 4:34 *My food is to do the will of the one who sent me and to* **finish** *his work.*

John 17:4 *I glorified you on earth by* **accomplishing** *the work that you gave me to do.*

John 19:28 *After this, aware that everything was now* **finished**, *in order that the scripture might be fulfilled, Jesus said, "I thirst."*

John 19:30 *When Jesus had taken the wine, he said, "It is* **finished.**" *And bowing his head, he handed over the spirit.*

Jesus was the fulfillment of the law, not its replacement, just as he says and modern day Pharisees demand. But the good news is that everything *has been accomplished*, through him.

Struggling against the legalism of simple obedience, we end by setting up the most dangerous law of all, the law of the world and the law of grace. In our effort to combat legalism we land ourselves in the worst kind of legalism. The only way of overcoming this legalism is by real obedience to Christ when he calls us to follow him; for in Jesus the law is at once fulfilled and cancelled.
Dietrich Bonhoeffer

DAY 4: JESUS RANSOMS US FROM THE LAW

But when the fullness of the time came, God sent forth His Son, born of a woman, born under the Law, so that He might redeem those who were under the Law, that we might receive the adoption as sons. Because you are sons, God has sent forth the Spirit of His Son into our hearts, crying, "Abba! Father!" Therefore you are no longer a slave, but a son; and if a son, then an heir through God. (Galatians 4:4-7 NASB)

This passage continues yesterday's reflection on Jesus' fulfillment, because the first line mentions "the fullness of time" coming. And so we return to our contemplation of jots and tittles briefly, while focusing on their most excellent replacement.

The book of Acts shows us various aspects of law were replaced by the freedom of Christ. Peter had a vision of a sheet like a movie screen being lowered in front of him. As a result, he proclaimed the rules had changed, and no animals were ineligible for consumption. Various epistles remind us even circumcision—the sign of the old covenant—was being dropped as a requirement of Christianity.

These were huge changes, and all of them are messages Christians should take to heart about what fulfillment of law means.

Paul tells us life under the law was a form of imprisonment. He says the law was a form of slavery. But when the fullness of time came and Jesus's mission was manifested, we were redeemed and adopted. His work of completing the law was finished, and we transformed from slaves to heirs.

Rejoice and know that in Christ the law has indeed been fulfilled.

Now I've been free, I know what a dreadful condition slavery is. I have seen hundreds of escaped slaves, but I never saw one who was willing to go back and be a slave.
Harriet Tubman

77

DAY 5: LOVE IS THE FULFILLING OF THE LAW

Owe no one anything, except to love each other, for the one who loves another has fulfilled the law. For the commandments, "You shall not commit adultery, You shall not murder, You shall not steal, You shall not covet," and any other commandment, are summed up in this word: "You shall love your neighbor as yourself." Love does no wrong to a neighbor; therefore love is the fulfilling of the law. (Romans 13:8-10 ESV)

For all his tendency toward legalism, Paul certainly got this right.

It's a passage which hardly warrants any additional commentary. You could simply read this three times, spend a few minutes in contemplation, and be done.

Love is the fulfilling of the law. Such simple words, and yet if you raise them to a non-affirming Christian you will get all sorts of pushback about what it means. For example, you'll hear that love means not leaving a friend in sin.

But how is it loving, under any circumstances, to tell someone they shouldn't be who they were born to be? How loving is it to tell a desperately lonely woman who is in fear of hell that she should remain alone forever rather than marry the woman who has brought wholeness to her being for the first time in her life? How is it loving to tell a teenager they can't perform gender in the way that is natural to them because their external sex characteristics don't match that gender?

Many Bible passages indicate slavery is socially acceptable. Would it be loving to tell a person held in slavery that God desires their suffering rather than their freedom? That's what fundamentalist leaning Christians do to their LGBTQI+ brothers and sisters when they tell them to deny who God created them to be. And it is wrong.

Paul reiterates Jesus' commandments to love one another. So go out and live the golden rule, and by doing so, fulfill the law. Treat your LGBTQI+ neighbors and family members the way you want to be treated.

What religion do I preach? The religion of love. The law of kindness brought to light by the gospel. What is this good for? To make all who receive it enjoy God and themselves, to make them like God, lovers of all, contented in their lives, and crying out at their death, in calm assurance, "O grave where is thy victory! Thanks be to God, who giveth me victory, through my Lord Jesus Christ."

John Wesley

DAY 6: RIGHTEOUSNESS COMES THROUGH JESUS

You have become estranged from Christ, you who attempt to be justified by law; you have fallen from grace. For we through the Spirit eagerly wait for the hope of righteousness by faith. For in Christ Jesus neither circumcision nor uncircumcision avails anything, but faith working through love.
(Galatians 5:4-6 NKJV)

There is something tremendously compelling about the idea that living according to law leads to righteousness. The scribes, Pharisees, and elders described in the gospels were so tormented by the need to protect the law they demanded Jesus' death. The young churches poor Paul wrote to endlessly fell prey to the same compulsion, as we see from today's reading.

In this fifth chapter of the letter, Paul counsels the young church in Galatia to return to the central truth of Christianity. He uses strong terms, saying they have become "estranged from Christ." The term "estranged" is typically applied to marital or familial relationships, and Paul expected them to have a more intimate relationship with Jesus than would permit the kind of straying he describes.

Unfortunately, this passage isn't merely an ancient artifact. What happened then isn't merely historical record. God breathed this letter not so we can look at the early church and laugh at their stubborn adherence to Judaism. The epistle is there because it is still relevant. We are still doing it.

When you encounter a conservative Christian who wants to talk to you about how Jesus' fulfillment of the law didn't negate adherence to that very law, suggest they read this passage and examine their hearts. Have they become estranged from Christ and returned to attempts at justification by law? Are they frustrating the Spirit, who eagerly waits for our hope of righteousness by faith?

The everlasting God has in His wisdom foreseen from eternity the cross that He now presents to you as a gift from His inmost heart. This cross He now sends you He has considered with His all-knowing eyes, understood with His divine mind, tested with His wise justice, warmed with loving arms and weighed with His own hands to see that it be not one inch too large and not one ounce too heavy for you. He has blessed it with His holy Name, anointed it with His consolation, taken one last glance at you and your courage, and then sent it to you from heaven, a special greeting from God to you, an alms of the all-merciful love of God.

St. Francis de Sales

DAY 7: LOVING GOD AND NEIGHBOR IS FULFILLMENT OF THE LAW

So the scribe said to Him, "Well said, Teacher. You have spoken the truth, for there is one God, and there is no other but He. And to love Him with all the heart, with all the understanding, with all the soul, and with all the strength, and to love one's neighbor as oneself, is more than all the whole burnt offerings and sacrifices."
Now when Jesus saw that he answered wisely, He said to him, "You are not far from the kingdom of God." (Mark 12:32-34 NKJV)

And behold, a certain lawyer stood up and tested Him, saying, "Teacher, what shall I do to inherit eternal life?" He said to him, "What is written in the law? What is your reading of it?" So he answered and said, "'You shall love the Lord your God with all your heart, with all your soul, with all your strength, and with all your mind,' and 'your neighbor as yourself.'" And He said to him, "You have answered rightly; do this and you will live." (Luke 10:25-28 NKJV)

We end this week as we started: by looking at Jesus commandments which consummate all those which came before.

As you move through this book you will encounter many examples of religious leaders being castigated by Jesus. But today we look at two readings which show religious experts exemplifying a proper understanding of faith. They struggled then, as we do now, with trying to understand how the message of Jesus Christ fits in with the message of the Hebrew Scriptures in which they were trained. In reading them, we see Jesus applauding their understanding that the new is bigger, greater, and more perfect than the old.

In seeing this, we return to the very first concept we examined: God is love. Jesus is the fulfillment of the law because Jesus is God, and God is love, and *love* is the law and the prophets.

Have you ever taken pride in your knowledge of the scriptures, and perhaps even used that knowledge to condemn LGBTQI+ people, even in your own mind? Take heart and turn, like the scribe in Mark's gospel above. There is still time for you to say along with him, that loving God and neighbor are more important than anything else. When you do so, you will not be far from the kingdom of God.

Jesus must not be read as having baited us with grace only to clobber us in the end with law. For as the death and resurrection of Jesus were accomplished once and for all, so the grace that reigns by those mysteries reigns eternally – even in the thick of judgment.

Robert Farrar Capon

CAN A SINNER BE CHRISTIAN?

"You can't be gay and call yourself Christian." The claim is made over and over again. It's based on the premise that same-sex behaviors and gender non-conformity are sinful, which is refuted later in this devotional. This week we look at what the scriptures say about the supposed sinlessness of Christians, so you are equipped to offer an answer next time you hear the proclamation.

DAY 1: JESUS CALLS HIS DISCIPLES EVIL

If you then, who are evil, know how to give good gifts to your children, how much more will your Father who is in heaven give good things to those who ask him! (Matthew 7: 11 ESV)

The question Christ poses in today's passage includes a central revelation; he calls the thousands of amassed followers listening to his Sermon on the Mount "evil." All of them; even his disciples. Remember, these are the people who knew Jesus best; the ones he later called friends. They walked beside him and learned from him. If you were one of that group, how do you think you would act? Wouldn't you be on your best behavior?

He doesn't qualify the statement by saying "those of you who do this or that are evil." He called them *all* evil. Other translations use the word "wicked," or "sinful," but the message is the same. Even though this band of believers was on fire with their new faith and in love with their savior friend, they still managed to sin.

Like us, they weren't all murders, thieves, or adulterers. But Jesus *does* warn that when we hate we commit murder, and when we lust we commit adultery. He knew then and knows now we are prone to envy, pride, covetousness, and lack of charity. We can't seem to help it. In this teaching, Jesus wants us to recognize we *all* fall short. All of those gathered back then, and all of us today. We should find this comforting. He loves us anyway, and urges us to ask the Father for good gifts, despite it.

Can a Christian be a sinner? According to Jesus, yes. Even those most close to him.

It is after you have realized that there is a real Moral Law, and a Power behind the law, and that you have broken that law and put yourself wrong with that Power — it is after all this, and not a moment sooner, that Christianity begins to talk.
C.S. Lewis

DAY 2: PAUL CALLS HIMSELF A SINNER

*Here is a trustworthy saying that deserves full acceptance: Christ Jesus
came into the world to save sinners—of whom I am the worst.*
(1 Timothy 1:16 NIV)

*I do not understand what I do. For what I want to do I do not do, but what I
hate I do. And if I do what I do not want to do, I agree that the law is good. As
it is, it is no longer I myself who do it, but it is sin living in me. For I know that
good itself does not dwell in me, that is, in my sinful nature. For I have the desire
to do what is good, but I cannot carry it out. For I do not do the good I want to
do, but the evil I do not want to do—this I keep on doing. Now if I do what I do
not want to do, it is no longer I who do it, but it is sin living in me that does it.*

*So I find this law at work: Although I want to do good, evil is right there
with me. For in my inner being I delight in God's law; but I see another law at
work in me, waging war against the law of my mind and making me a prisoner of
the law of sin at work within me. What a wretched man I am! Who will rescue
me from this body that is subject to death? Thanks be to God, who delivers me
through Jesus Christ our Lord!* (Romans 7:15-25 NIV)

St. Paul is an interesting person. He is the hero of fundamentalist-
leaning Christians who point to him with great fury and agitation
when they want to decry the mote of dust in their brother's eye. They
demand the passages in which Paul points out various sinful
behaviors prove sinners don't make it to heaven. They ignore the
logs in their own eyes which Paul describes. They also ignore this
passage, in which Paul says that despite having an encounter with
Christ which literally knocked him off his high horse, he remained a
sinner.

Some try to say Paul put all of that sin stuff behind him, but these
passages are clear. He says he kept on doing it.

Like him we look to the last line of these verses: *Thanks be to God,
who delivers me through Jesus Christ our Lord!*

If my sinfulness appears to me to be in any way smaller or less detestable in comparison with the sins of others, I am still not recognizing my sinfulness at all. ... How can I possibly serve another person in unfeigned humility if I seriously regard his sinfulness as worse than my own?

Dietrich Bonhoeffer

DAY 3: JESUS CALLS PETER SATAN

*Simon Peter answered, "You are the Christ, the Son of the living God."
And Jesus said to him, "Blessed are you, Simon Barjona, because flesh
and blood did not reveal this to you, but My Father who is in heaven. I
also say to you that you are Peter, and upon this rock I will build My
church; and the gates of Hades will not overpower it. I will give you the
keys of the kingdom of heaven; and whatever you bind on earth shall have
been bound in heaven, and whatever you loose on earth shall have been
loosed in heaven." Then He warned the disciples that they should tell no
one that He was the Christ.*

*From that time Jesus began to show His disciples that He must go to
Jerusalem, and suffer many things from the elders and chief priests and
scribes, and be killed, and be raised up on the third day. Peter took Him
aside and began to rebuke Him, saying, "God forbid it, Lord! This shall
never happen to You." But He turned and said to Peter, "Get behind Me,
Satan! You are a stumbling block to Me; for you are not setting your
mind on God's interests, but man's."* (Matthew 16:16-23 NASB)

Peter was an impetuous man when it came to defending his friend
and teacher. In the garden of Gethsemane, he cut off the ear of the
high priest's servant. In today's passage he displays that impetuosity
by telling Jesus he won't let him be killed.

Jesus' response is strong; he calls Peter Satan!

Remember, this isn't just any Christian. Jesus is speaking about
Simon Peter; the man upon whom Jesus pledges to build his church.
Remember also that even as Jesus was renaming Simon "Rock," he
knew he'd be calling him Satan a few minutes later. He knew Peter
would pick up the sword in the grief-filled garden and cut the ear off
of a servant. He knew Peter would offer three fireside denials on his
way to the cross.

Yet despite Jesus' knowledge of these things and of all Peter's
sinfulness, he named him Rock, and pledged to build his church
upon him.

We know to whom much has been given, much is required. Peter was given a very special place in the formation of the early church. He was lavished with love and attention from Jesus, as part of his trio of closest friends. Many things must have been required from Peter in response, however, sinlessness was not one of them.

If only it were all so simple! If only there were evil people somewhere insidiously committing evil deeds, and it were necessary only to separate them from the rest of us and destroy them. But the line dividing good and evil cuts through the heart of every human being. And who is willing to destroy a piece of his own heart?
Aleksandr Solzhenitsyn

DAY 4: JOHN TELLS US WHAT TO DO WHEN WE SIN

My little children, I am writing this to you so that you may not sin; but if any one does sin, we have an advocate with the Father, Jesus Christ the righteous; and he is the expiation for our sins, and not for ours only but also for the sins of the whole world. (1 John 2:1-2 RSV)

Today's passage pretty thoroughly blows the idea that Christians don't sin right out of the water.

This is John, writing to the new believers. His words don't echo our modern-day religious experts who proclaim that humans are somehow perfected simply by praying the sinners' prayer. Quite the opposite. He acknowledges that Christians *will* sin, because we are all children of Adam and Eve, like them in our willingness to act out of fear or selfishness rather than out of love. We are all periodic tasters of forbidden fruit, blame shifters, and doubters of God's provision. We won't be perfected until we stand before God through death; naked and stripped of all ungodly leanings.

So yes, we will sin, as the beloved disciple points out. And more importantly, we have one who is our advocate with the Father. He is the one like us in all things, understanding our temptations, and explaining our weaknesses.

Can Christians sin? Of course, which is why Our Father sent Jesus: to show he loves us anyway.

Rebuke no one, revile no one, not even men who live very wickedly. Spread your cloak over the man who is falling and cover him. And if you cannot take upon yourself his sins and receive his chastisement in his stead, then at least patiently suffer his shame and do not disgrace him.

St. Isaac the Syrian

DAY 5: JESUS PRAISES A WORSHIPPER OF MANY GODS

When Jesus had entered Capernaum, a centurion came to him, asking for help. "Lord," he said, "my servant lies at home paralyzed, suffering terribly." Jesus said to him, "Shall I come and heal him?" The centurion replied, "Lord, I do not deserve to have you come under my roof. But just say the word, and my servant will be healed. For I myself am a man under authority, with soldiers under me. I tell this one, 'Go,' and he goes; and that one, 'Come,' and he comes. I say to my servant, 'Do this,' and he does it." When Jesus heard this, he was amazed and said to those following him, "Truly I tell you, I have not found anyone in Israel with such great faith. I say to you that many will come from the east and the west, and will take their places at the feast with Abraham, Isaac and Jacob in the kingdom of heaven." (Matthew 8:5-11 NIV)

Centurions were officers in the Roman military who commanded groups of soldiers called "legionaries." Responsibilities included training, assigning work details, and administering discipline. They were paid much more than a normal soldier, and were powerful and highly respected. However, they were Romans, and Romans were polytheistic, meaning they worshipped multiple gods.

The Ten Commandments and nearly all the books of the Bible contain warnings about idolatry. Hundreds of passages describe God's wrath against idolaters. In the epistles, Paul repeatedly warns against slipping back into the ways of those who worship the old gods. Given his military responsibilities, the centurion in this passage was probably a devotee of Mars, the god of war. From a polytheistic viewpoint, he would have had no problem adding a new entity into his personal pantheon. He heard of Jesus and believed. He acknowledged that Jesus' power was so great he could simply speak a command of deliverance and healing, and the servant would be freed, from miles away.

The centurion was undoubtedly an idolatrous sinner of the kind decried throughout scriptures, and yet look at Jesus' amazed words. He says he had not found such faith among the "faithful" of Israel.

He said many like that idolater would participate in the heavenly feast.

We will all be wrong about many things in our lifetime. We will sin. But God doesn't expect perfection. He desires our yearning for his will, and for love, and for faith.

The sinners to whom Jesus directed His messianic ministry were not those who skipped morning devotions or Sunday church. His ministry was to those whom society considered real sinners. They had done nothing to merit salvation. Yet they opened themselves to the gift that was offered them. On the other hand, the self-righteous placed their trust in the works of the Law and closed their hearts to the message of grace.

Brennan Manning

DAY 6: TAX COLLECTORS AND PROSTITUTES ENTER HEAVEN

Jesus entered the temple courts, and, while he was teaching, the chief priests and the elders of the people came to him. "By what authority are you doing these things?" they asked. "And who gave you this authority?"

Jesus said to them, "Truly I tell you, the tax collectors and the prostitutes are entering the kingdom of God ahead of you. For John came to you to show you the way of righteousness, and you did not believe him, but the tax collectors and the prostitutes did. And even after you saw this, you did not repent and believe him. (Matthew 21:23, 31-32 NIV)

The religious authorities of Jesus' day walked in pride, believing they knew all about what God wanted and how to make him happy. A great percentage of the gospels are Jesus' tireless attempts to get them to realize they were wrong. Today's passage is one more example.

Jesus mentions two despised groups—prostitutes and tax collectors—to try to rattle the chief priests and elders off their high and mighty perches. By their rules, prostitutes and tax collectors should *never* make it to heaven.

And yet Jesus' response is clear: the rules had changed. Love and mercy were the new commandments which overrode all others. Those who believed that truth, regardless of their lot in life or their standing within the religious community, were entering the kingdom of God.

They continue to do so today. How weary God must be with today's chief priests and elders demanding their righteousness, and denying that Love is truly the answer?

Nothing that we despise in other men is inherently absent from ourselves. We must learn to regard people less in the light of what they do or don't do, and more in light of what they suffer.
Dietrich Bonhoeffer

DAY 7: IF WE CLAIM TO BE WITHOUT SIN WE DECEIVE OURSELVES

For we have already made the charge that Jews and Gentiles alike are all under the power of sin. As it is written: "There is no one righteous, not even one" (Romans 3:9-10 NIV)

For there is no distinction, since all have sinned and fall short of the glory of God; they are now justified by his grace as a gift, through the redemption that is in Christ Jesus, whom God put forward as a sacrifice of atonement by his blood, effective through faith.
(Romans 3:22-25 NRSV)

If we claim to be without sin, we deceive ourselves and the truth is not in us. If we confess our sins, he is faithful and just and will forgive us our sins and purify us from all unrighteousness. If we claim we have not sinned, we make him out to be a liar and his word is not in us.
(1 John 1:8-10 NIV)

Today is our last day of examining whether or not Christians can be sinners. We end it like a fireworks display, with multiple pops and bangs firing at once, though in this case, the rockets are scripture passages.

The first thing to remember is that the epistles weren't written to non-believers who the authors would *expect* to sin. They are addressed to the leaders of various churches; the experts in Christianity at the time. And apparently those leaders needed correction in their understanding of this very issue, because both John and Paul felt the need to make it clear we are *all* sinners. Paul points out that in fact, there are no distinctions. He is trying to get the church in Rome to stop making distinctions because the reality of our nature is singular.

But John's words should rattle the bones of any modern day church leader or Pharisee who demands LGBTQI+ persons can't be Christian because of their supposed sinfulness. If those people try to claim Christians are not sinners, John says they are making Jesus out to be a liar, and his word is not in them.

We all fall, and we are all justified through the miraculous gift of Jesus. Pretending otherwise is a slap in the face of the Christ.

> *Now I wonder whether I have sufficiently realized that during all this time God has been trying to find me, to know me, and to love me. The question is not "How am I to find God?" but "How am I to let myself be found by him?" The question is not "How am I to know God?" but "How am I to let myself be known by God?" And, finally, the question is not "How am I to love God?" but "How am I to let myself be loved by God?" God is looking into the distance for me, trying to find me, and longing to bring me home.*
>
> Henri J.M. Nouwen

WHO DOES JESUS CONDEMN AND WHY?

Our previous readings have revealed that Jesus was quite a rebel, and radically inclusive. So did he chastise anyone? The answer is yes, and you'll see who those people were as we continue our studies this week.

DAY 1: THOSE WHO SHUT THE DOOR OF HEAVEN

"Woe to you, teachers of the law and Pharisees, you hypocrites! You shut the door of the kingdom of heaven in people's faces." "And so upon you will come all the righteous blood that has been shed on earth"
(Matthew 23:13, 35 NIV)

Jesus was harsh to only two groups: those who turned his father's house into a marketplace, and the scribes and Pharisees, who blocked the way to the kingdom and bore their religiosity like a golden hammer.

Evangelical Christians tend toward a Bible-alone theology, and tend to believe the scriptures are evergreen in their entirety. As discussed previously, the belief generally seems to be that all the rules presented still apply (except in the case of things like haircuts, fabric composition, stoning, and dozens of others dismissively lumped into "Old Covenant.")

But this brand of modern Christian dismisses Jesus' woes to the Pharisees in today's passage from Matthew 23, apparently deeming them merely historical. Perhaps snickering at those persnickety Pharisees, who counted cumin seeds and nagged about tiny bugs in the meager wine cups of the poor. These moderns feel good about what they believe is their own simpler relationship, based on faith alone, and seem to think if Jesus' woes apply to anyone, it's to the Roman Catholics.

This is exactly the kind of viperish hypocrisy which Jesus condemned. Out of one side of the pulpit we hear that all of the scriptures continue to apply to Christians today: all the parables, all Paul's warnings about sin, and most especially those few mentions of same-sex relations.

But fist-bangers in that same pulpit don't seem to think Jesus' woes should be viewed as a warning to God's people today. And that seems exceedingly odd, given the unprecedented harshness of Jesus' stance, and the sheer force of his derisive disapproval.

Jesus never speaks to anyone in the scriptures that way again. It's to this group of rule-wielding "God defenders" alone that he unleashes the full force of his verbal condemnation. And this warning is evergreen. He's still unleashing his disapproval on those who continue to do it today.

Every time we use religion to draw a line to keep people out, Jesus is with the people on the other side of that line.

Hugh L. Hollowell

DAY 2: NEGLECTORS OF JUSTICE, MERCY, AND FAITH

"Woe to you, scribes and Pharisees, hypocrites! For you tithe mint, dill, and cummin, and have neglected the weightier matters of the law: justice and mercy and faith. It is these you ought to have practiced without neglecting the others. You blind guides! You strain out a gnat but swallow a camel!" (Matthew 23:23-24 NRSVCE)

It's surprising that our modern day scribes and Pharisees don't quake in fear. Remember yesterday's mention of spices? Jesus' woes are quite clear, and they are repeated. The religious elites feel good about doing the lesser things: going to church, tithing, praying before dinner. But today's words from Jesus aren't simply historical artifacts. They are intended to pierce our very souls. They should convict us to always strive for deeper faith, lived out more fully. He calls justice and mercy "weightier matters of the law," and that means for us as well as for those long-dead religious experts.

It can be hard to know how to address a loved one who is caught up in Pharisaical thinking. They are generally so quick to draw out scripture passages as weapons, ready to cut off efforts to speak love and truth. But what you *can* do is remind them of this verse. Ask them to consider what justice means for the same-sex couple who wants to celebrate God's bringing them together by marrying in church. Or what it means for the transgender youth who wants to use the bathroom with the other guys. Or what it means for the family of a transgender woman who worries she will be murdered in the street. Ask them what mercy looks like for these people, in these circumstances. Then ask them to do appropriate actions of mercy in response.

There's a good chance they won't be able to hear you. But you can try. And know Jesus himself will be watching in approval, and cheering you on.

Jesus condemned no one except hypocrites.
Kallistos Ware

DAY 3: PROPHET KILLERS

"You snakes! You brood of vipers! How will you escape being condemned to hell? Therefore I am sending you prophets and sages and teachers. Some of them you will kill and crucify; others you will flog in your synagogues and pursue from town to town." (Matthew 23:33-34 NIV)

The traditional Christian view of prophets comes from the Hebrew Scriptures, with John the Baptist bringing up the tail end. Most Christians think John was the last prophet. This crowd of faith heroes preached repentance and a turning away from other gods. They beseeched the Jews to turn back lest they be consumed by fire, flood, and pestilence.

But in today's scripture Jesus tells us he will send prophets, sages, and teachers, so apparently John the Baptist was not the last.

Just as in the days before he came, Jesus continues to send speakers of God's truths to the religious who refuse to listen. The voices are all around us. One might even be your own child, who tries to open your unwittingly Pharisaical heart to truths you've not allowed yourself to embrace. Perhaps your daughter has tried to explain why your views on gender are narrow-minded and culturally inflicted. Perhaps she told stories of good friends who are transgender. Perhaps she disagreed vehemently with your theories about the causes and social ramifications of homosexuality. Or maybe it was your son, or a sister you don't talk to any more.

Sometimes these prophets might even be atheists, who recognize what love looks like and point out actions of exclusion and condemnation when they see it.

Before Saul was knocked off his horse and became Paul, he was a persecutor of truth and a crucifier of prophets. He was sincere, and he was wrong. How much must he have regretted the stoning of Stephen throughout the years until his own death?

Let's pray we don't require such drastic measures and can recognize the prophets, sages, and teachers Jesus sends to beseech us to repent our lack of love.

Lilies that fester smell far worse than weeds.
William Shakespeare

DAY 4: BLIND PHARISEES

Then Jesus said, "I came into this world for judgment, so that those who do not see might see, and those who do see might become blind." Some of the Pharisees who were with him heard this and said to him, "Surely we are not also blind, are we?" Jesus said to them, "If you were blind, you would have no sin; but now you are saying, 'We see,' so your sin remains. (John 9:39-41 NABRE)

John's phrasing often tends toward the mystical and can be confusing. The words of Jesus in today's passage are a good example; with the blind not sinning and those with sight not actually seeing at all.

Let's look at the verses in another translation. This time, they come from *The Message*:

Jesus then said, "I came into the world to bring everything into the clear light of day, making all the distinctions clear, so that those who have never seen will see, and those who have made a great pretense of seeing will be exposed as blind." Some Pharisees overheard him and said, "Does that mean you're calling us blind?" Jesus said, "If you were really blind, you would be blameless, but since you claim to see everything so well, you're accountable for every fault and failure." (John 9:39-41 MSG)

This is powerful clarification. In many ways, it is the condensation of this whole devotional.

Jesus came to bring clarity about what God wants. In these verses he brings the wrong-headed view about law over love into the clear light of day, and calls it blindness. Not just that; he warns that those who claim to have great insight into righteousness (as dependent on law) are to be held accountable for every fault and failure. The blind, those who don't make proclamations about the requirements for God's approval, will be blameless.

You have a choice today, and every day. You can live your life by claiming to see God's judgment and wrath over others with perfect clarity, based on the Bible which describes him. Or you can live by the model of Christ; blind behind the darkened glass, and simply trusting in his love and mercy.

> *If my activism, however well-motivated, drives out love, then I have misunderstood Jesus' gospel. I am stuck with law, not the gospel of grace.*
>
> Philip Yancey

DAY 5: PRIDEFUL PHARISEES

To some who were confident of their own righteousness and looked down on everyone else, Jesus told this parable: "Two men went up to the temple to pray, one a Pharisee and the other a tax collector. The Pharisee stood by himself and prayed: 'God, I thank you that I am not like other people— robbers, evildoers, adulterers—or even like this tax collector. I fast twice a week and give a tenth of all I get.'

"But the tax collector stood at a distance. He would not even look up to heaven, but beat his breast and said, 'God, have mercy on me, a sinner.' "I tell you that this man, rather than the other, went home justified before God. For all those who exalt themselves will be humbled, and those who humble themselves will be exalted." (Luke 18:9-14 NIV)

LGBTQI+ individuals face the attitude of the Pharisee all the time, though it isn't always stated as starkly as in this parable. By condemning what they believe to be sinful feelings or actions on the part of LGBTQI+ people, modern fundamentalist-leaning Christians proclaim their own righteousness. Perhaps they even pray like this Pharisee: "God, I thank you that I am not like other people—gays, lesbians, and transgender persons."

Tax collecting wasn't a sinful occupation, just as being LGBTQI+ isn't a sinful state of being. But many tax collectors acted unethically. Like every human—gay, straight, non-binary, cisgender, and everything in between—they were sinners. But notice, Jesus tells this parable to show us that considering our own state of sinfulness to be less than others is something he denounces.

Remember to pray for your fundamentalist-leaning Christian brothers and sisters, that they may humble themselves before God, and in doing so, be exalted.

Those who love their dream of a Christian community more than they love the Christian community itself become destroyers of that Christian community even though their personal intentions may be ever so honest, earnest and sacrificial. God hates this wishful dreaming because it makes the dreamer proud and pretentious. Those who dream of this idolized community demand that it be fulfilled by God, by others and by

themselves. They enter the community of Christians with their demands set up by their own law, and judge one another and God accordingly.
Dietrich Bonhoeffer

DAY 6: DENIERS OF ACCESS TO GOD

Since the Passover of the Jews was near, Jesus went up to Jerusalem. He found in the temple area those who sold oxen, sheep, and doves, as well as the money-changers seated there. He made a whip out of cords and drove them all out of the temple area, with the sheep and oxen, and spilled the coins of the money-changers and overturned their tables, and to those who sold doves he said, "Take these out of here, and stop making my Father's house a marketplace." His disciples recalled the words of scripture, "Zeal for your house will consume me." (John 2:13-17 NABRE)

The second chapter of John's gospel opens with the wedding at Cana, showing us that Jesus' first miraculous action was purely a gift of love and joy: wine for the people gathered to celebrate a wedding. John then moves on to show us an angry Christ.

The money changers and animal purveyors were nothing new to Jesus. As devout Jews, his family would have dutifully traveled to Jerusalem each year for Passover. He knew the abusers of his Father's house would be there this year as well, and so he prepared by tying together cords for specific use as a whip. His fury was premeditated.

Some say he was just mad that people were making money in the temple. But Jesus has never been terribly concerned about money. What he *is* concerned about is people. In this scenario, year after year, people were earnestly trying to obey the law by offering sacrifices at Passover. Many traveled long distances to be there, wanting to meet God in his sanctuary. But those who changed money at a price and sold animals at inflated costs were a barrier. For some of the faithful, the cost they exacted was too high, and kept them from entering.

Conservative Christians perform that same function today. When their LGBTQI+ brothers and sisters long to be obedient Christians by showing up at church to worship God, they are asked to deny their identities. To deny their very being.

Jesus brandished whips at those who exacted too high a price for access to God's house. He cannot be happy with those who continue to do so.

We do not see Jesus condemning the sinners in the world; rather, he condemns the leaders of God's people with his severest words.

Jerram Barrs

DAY 7: THOSE WHO WILL NOT PRODUCE GOOD FRUIT

But when he saw many of the Pharisees and Sadducees coming to where he was baptizing, he said to them: "You brood of vipers! Who warned you to flee from the coming wrath? Produce fruit in keeping with repentance. And do not think you can say to yourselves, 'We have Abraham as our father.' I tell you that out of these stones God can raise up children for Abraham. The ax is already at the root of the trees, and every tree that does not produce good fruit will be cut down and thrown into the fire.
(Matthew 3:7-10 NIV)

From the earliest days of Jesus' ministry, the warnings rang out. In today's case the warning comes through the voice of John the Baptist. He calls the religious elite a "brood of vipers," which is a phrase Jesus echoed in verses we looked at earlier this week. John tried to warn them they need to change their mode of thinking, because it isn't what God wants. The Pharisees and Sadducees (along with their modern-day counterparts) thought they had the path to righteousness all sewn up based on their study of the scriptures and theoretical adherence to the law. But they weren't producing good fruit:

But the fruit of the Spirit is love, joy, peace, forbearance, kindness, goodness, faithfulness, gentleness and self-control. (Galatians 5:22-23 NIV)

Do you know any Christians who fall into the same camp?

Some of the Pharisees and Sadducees listened to John's warning, and did indeed repent. Others continued to demand God was a harsh taskmaster who determined our eternal destinies based on how closely we followed the particular sets of rules and regulations they determined to be required. They didn't hear what John was trying to tell them. Perhaps they couldn't hear.

Matthew tells us God could raise up believers out of the very stones themselves. If he can do that, he most certainly can raise up children for Jesus from amongst the LGBTQI+ community. And he will most certainly revel in the fruit they bear.

The causes of my uneasiness are these: 1. The lack of spiritual fruit in the lives of so many who claim to have faith. 2. The rarity of a radical change in the conduct and general outlook of persons professing their new faith in Christ as their personal Saviour....Plain horse sense ought to tell us that anything that makes no change in the man who professes it makes no difference to God either, and it is an easily observable fact that for countless numbers of persons the change from no-faith to faith makes no actual difference in the life.

A.W. Tozer

WHAT DOES JESUS ASK US TO DO?

We've learned a lot about God, the law, and Jesus as rebel iconoclast. But what is it he *wants* us to do? How does he want us to act as Christians? This week we dive deep into the waters pouring from the side of Christ to understand better what he desires from his followers.

DAY 1: WORSHIP IN SPIRIT AND TRUTH

The woman said to him, "Sir, I can see that you are a prophet. Our
ancestors worshiped on this mountain; but you people say that the place to
worship is in Jerusalem." Jesus said to her, "Believe me, woman, the hour
is coming when you will worship the Father neither on this mountain nor
in Jerusalem. You people worship what you do not understand; we worship
what we understand, because salvation is from the Jews. But the hour is
coming, and is now here, when true worshipers will worship the Father in
Spirit and truth; and indeed the Father seeks such people to worship him.
God is Spirit, and those who worship him must worship in Spirit and
truth." (John 4:19-24 NABRE)

In today's passage we find Jesus talking to a Samaritan woman at
Jacob's well, where he's stopped for a drink on his walk back from
Judea to Galilee. They are nearing the end of their conversation, and
the woman seeks spiritual wisdom from him, not yet realizing he is,
in fact, the Messiah.

She was surprised he would talk with her at all. Samaritans were
despised by Jews for not following the customs of the law as the Jews
believed they should. The woman brought up the issue of where
sacrifices were to be offered; at the temple on Mt. Gerizim, or in
Jerusalem. Despite knowing a Jewish man would disdain her, both
for being a Samaritan and for her history with men, she sought
knowledge from him. She sought truth. She wanted to know what the
right way to worship really was.

Jesus' response is profound. He didn't tell her which was the right
place to worship. Quite the contrary; he talked about "true" worship.
True worship is not about the rules of place and laws of behavior. He
pointed out that God is Spirit, and said we are to worship in Spirit
and truth.

Worshiping in Spirit is an action of union, in which the Holy Spirit
implanted within us reaches out to join with the Spirit of the Trinity.
It is experiential rather than cognitive. It is a matter of heart and will
rather than of thought and reason. It is an act of opening and
reaching rather than reading and preaching. When we worship in the

Spirit we are erasing our own boundaries in order to better merge with God's boundlessness.

This is not possible when we demand that worship take place on a particular site or be constrained by the pages of a book, no matter how holy. To do so we have to acknowledge what Jesus told us; the Father desires us to join with him, Spirit to Spirit. Wordless, placeless, and without boundaries.

I wept at the beauty of your hymns and canticles, and was powerfully moved at the sweet sound of your Church singing. These sounds flowed into my ears, and the truth streamed into my heart.

St. Augustine of Hippo

DAY 2: SEEK UNITY

I ask not only on behalf of these, but also on behalf of those who will
believe in me through their word, that they may all be one. As you, Father,
are in me and I am in you, may they also be in us, so that the world may
believe that you have sent me. The glory that you have given me I have
given them, so that they may be one, as we are one, I in them and you in
me, that they may become completely one, so that the world may know that
you have sent me and have loved them even as you have loved me. Father, I
desire that those also, whom you have given me, may be with me where I
am, to see my glory, which you have given me because you loved me before
the foundation of the world. Righteous Father, the world does not know
you, but I know you; and these know that you have sent me. I made your
name known to them, and I will make it known, so that the love with
which you have loved me may be in them, and I in them.
(John 17:20-26 NRSV)

Many young people who desire faithfulness to God are moving away from Christianity because of the condemnation toward the LGBTQI+ community doled out by various denominations. They want communion with the person of Christ but don't know how to find it within bodies which exclude members based on their sexual or gender identity.

Perhaps even sadder are the millions of atheists who watch such discrimination unfold in Jesus' name. Their derision of faith is confirmed because any being who approves of that behavior while claiming to be the God of love is a liar and a hypocrite.

Discussions about LGBTQI+ issues on Christian conservative social media sites and web pages read like a lesson from C.S. Lewis' *Screwtape Letters*. You can picture the babbling of hundreds of self-congratulatory Christians, proclaiming hellfire and brimstone and gleefully rubbing their Bible-ink-smeared hands together. This is probably what one corner of hell looks and sounds like.

Is it any wonder the world does not recognize divinity within the church?

Today's reading is Jesus' prayer for us, his new church. He prayed for our unity; our supernatural oneness. He has given us the glory the

Father passed on to him. He has loved us as the Father loved him. He desires our oneness in return.

To what end? So the world may know God.

You are the main character in the story of your life, but other people are the main characters of their own lives. And sometimes you can find healing just by playing a supporting role in someone else's experience.

Timothy Kurek

DAY 3: DO JUSTICE

Is not this the fast that I choose: to loose the bonds of injustice, to undo the thongs of the yoke, to let the oppressed go free, and to break every yoke? Is it not to share your bread with the hungry, and bring the homeless poor into your house; when you see the naked, to cover them, and not to hide yourself from your own kin? Then your light shall break forth like the dawn, and your healing shall spring up quickly; your vindicator shall go before you, the glory of the Lord shall be your rear guard. Then you shall call, and the Lord will answer; you shall cry for help, and he will say, Here I am. (Isaiah 58:6-9 NRSVCE)

It begins in the Hebrew Scriptures, the lovely picture of what God desires for our behavior as faithful followers of the one who *is* Love.

In Isaiah's day, the Jewish people followed the letter of the law about fasting, but the prophet's words show us it wasn't what God wanted. *His* fast was actions of social justice: to feed the hungry; to free the oppressed; to untie those who are burdened by the yoke of the past; to loose the bonds of injustice.

Members of the LGBTQI+ community have been oppressed for generations and continue to be oppressed today. They are hunched over, ashamed, denied rights, and excluded. Many are even tortured and killed.

Isaiah repeatedly points to the coming of Jesus, who multiplies these demands for social justice in his own teaching, and who demonstrates them in his actions. And look at the promise to those who step up and break apart those bonds and help free the oppressed! Your light shall break forth, healing shall spring up, and God Himself will be your glory and your guard. He will answer your cries for help, and he will be with you.

If you remove the yoke from among you, the accusing finger, and malicious speech; if you lavish your food on the hungry and satisfy the afflicted; then your light shall rise in the darkness, and your gloom shall become like midday; then the Lord will guide you always and satisfy your thirst in parched places, will give strength to your bones and you shall be like a

watered garden, like a flowing spring whose waters never fail. (Isaiah
58:9b-11 NABRE)

Unless we do his teachings, we do not demonstrate faith in him.
Ezra Taft Benson

DAY 4: WASH FEET

One of the Pharisees asked Jesus to eat with him, and he went into the Pharisee's house and took his place at the table. And a woman in the city, who was a sinner, having learned that he was eating in the Pharisee's house, brought an alabaster jar of ointment. She stood behind him at his feet, weeping, and began to bathe his feet with her tears and to dry them with her hair. Then she continued kissing his feet and anointing them with the ointment. Now when the Pharisee who had invited him saw it, he said to himself, "If this man were a prophet, he would have known who and what kind of woman this is who is touching him—that she is a sinner."
(Luke7:36-39 NRSVCE)

There is no greater scene of intimacy in the New Testament scriptures than this one. Here we have Jesus, lying down at a table in the house of presumably holy men, when a woman appears. Perhaps she is adorned with the scarlet letter of her day. She enters carrying a sign of her wealth: expensive ointment, possibly earned through acts of prostitution. But she enters bravely, intent on lavishing her love on Jesus despite knowing her unworthiness, and despite the ridicule and abuse she would face from the men who were gathered there.

It was immediately clear she hadn't just dropped in to say hello. She performed an act both intimate and humble, crying and kissing and drying his feet with her hair. Lubricating and massaging each tired foot with her hands.

Imagine the love and tenderness with which she must have touched him. Imagine the courage it must have taken for her to do it. Imagine Jesus' reaction to such a brave and loving affirmation.

Jesus did not respond well to the accusations of his host. He rebuked the man.

This sinful woman and her taboo action had a profound effect on Jesus. Her acts of love spoke to him so powerfully he repeated it at the last supper, when he washed the apostles' feet and instructed them to do the same.

Our Christ does not shun social pariahs. Quite the opposite. As this example shows us, he sometimes even imitates them.

Most of us prefer to eat with people who are like us, with shared background, values, socioeconomic status, ethnicity, beliefs, and tastes, or perhaps with people we want to be like, people who make us feel important and esteemed. Just as a bad ingredient may contaminate a meal, we often fear bad company may contaminate our reputation or our comfort. This is why Jesus' critics repeatedly drew attention to the fact that he dined with tax collectors and sinners. By eating with the poor, the despised, the sick, the sinners, the outcasts, and the unclean, Jesus was saying, "These are my companions. These are my friends." It was just the sort of behavior that got him killed.

Rachel Held Evans

DAY 5: BE LIKE CHILDREN

At that time the disciples came to Jesus, saying, "Who then is greatest in the kingdom of heaven?"

Then Jesus called a little child to Him, set him in the midst of them, and said, "Assuredly, I say to you, unless you are converted and become as little children, you will by no means enter the kingdom of heaven. Therefore whoever humbles himself as this little child is the greatest in the kingdom of heaven. (Matthew 18:1-4 NKJV)

In our enlightened age, we strive to prove our religious worth through knowledge; of scripture, of theology, of many things. We somehow think displaying how much we know shows the sincerity of our faith.

You might come up against this kind of mindset in your attempts to defend the right for LGBTQI+ individuals to participate fully in the life of the church. You might be battered by a barrage of scripture passages without getting a chance to respond or even take a breath. You might be hammered with facts from the tradition of a particular denomination backed up by centuries-old efforts to separate and exclude.

But Jesus tells us this sort of prideful demonstration of knowledge isn't what he wants, and certainly isn't something he requires. Instead, he wants us to approach him like a child. And what are the characteristics of childlike humility? Trust. A desire to lean in and hear. Love. Affection. Faith that you will be cared for.

So the next time you are hammered with law, scripture, and "church teaching," remember who Jesus calls us to be. Then be that.

Those who keep speaking about the sun while walking under a cloudy sky are messengers of hope, the true saints of our day.
Henri Nouwen

DAY 6: KEEP HIS COMMANDMENTS

"If you love me, keep my commandments." "If anyone loves me, he will keep my word. Then my Father will love him, and we will go to him and make our home within him. The one who doesn't love me doesn't keep my words. The words that you're hearing me say are not mine, but come from the Father who sent me." (John 14:15, 23-24 ISV)

Wouldn't it be wonderful if we had Jesus at our side to explain his words? We don't have him bodily with us, but Jesus promised to send the Holy Spirit to guide us and shine revelation into our hearts and minds. He is generous in responding when we ask for his presence. For today's contemplation, let the Spirit shine light on the first sentence, and in particular, on the word "my."

Jesus doesn't say listeners should follow what Moses commanded. In this final discourse to his apostles, Jesus doesn't hammer them with the need for strict adherence to the law. He doesn't mention law at all, in fact. He discusses only the need for love, and the encouragement the Holy Spirit will provide in the dark days which will follow when Jesus is no longer physically among them.

Jesus indeed offers us a new commandment, and as we see in glorious detail throughout the gospels, that commandment subsumes the law and the prophets. Today he asks us to keep *his* commandments.

When you choose love over what conservative Christian voices deem to be Old-Testament-Father-breathed rules and regulations, be at peace. The Father sent Jesus to speak a new thing. He is the new Word.

Jesus himself is our new commandment.

True religion is a union of God with the soul, a real participation of the divine nature, the very image of God drawn upon the soul, or in the apostle's phrase, it is Christ formed in us.

Henry Scougal

DAY 7: LOVE YOURSELF

*"You shall love the Lord your God with all your heart and with all your
soul and with all your mind. This is the great and first commandment.
And a second is like it: You shall love your neighbor as yourself."*
(Matthew 22:37-39 ESV)

This is not the first time we have addressed the words of Jesus about
the greatest commandments. It comes up in various places in this
devotional because of the power of the statements, and because of
the layers of meaning within them.

Today we focus on the last line. In fact, the last word.

Jesus is saying something very important in the phrase "You shall
love your neighbor as yourself." When reading this, we generally
focus on the outward. We realize we need to be forgiving, charitable,
caring, accepting, and generous with our neighbor. But if we limit our
focus to the beginning of the sentence, we miss a crucial piece.

Jesus is telling us we have to love *ourselves.* The second
commandment he offers is really two. In order to love others as
ourselves, we must love ourselves. We must value ourselves, care for
ourselves, forgive ourselves, accept ourselves, and be generous with
ourselves.

God comes to love us, just as we are. Straight, gay, lesbian, queer,
bi, transgender, intersex, non-binary, whatever. And he needs us to
love ourselves, just as we are, so we are able to love others.

*God loves human beings. God loves the world. Not an ideal human, but
human beings as they are; not an ideal world, but the real world. What we
find repulsive in their opposition to God, what we shrink back from with
pain and hostility, namely, real human beings, the real world, this is for
God the ground of unfathomable love.*
Dietrich Bonhoeffer

MALE AND FEMALE, HE CREATED THEM

As we near the end of the book, we finally reach the topics which ultra-conservative Christians both obsess about and fear: gender and sexuality. But there's nothing to be afraid of. Sexual and gender identities, in all their rainbow hues, are reflections of the person of Christ.

To kick off this three week study, we examine the mystery of male and female through the lens of scripture.

DAY 1: MALE AND FEMALE HE CREATED THEM

Then God said, "Let us make mankind in our image, in our likeness, so that they may rule over the fish in the sea and the birds in the sky, over the livestock and all the wild animals, and over all the creatures that move along the ground." So God created mankind in his own image, in the image of God he created them; male and female he created them.
(Genesis 1:26-27 NIV)

Most of us miss the full import of this passage. We focus on the binary and read it as God having made us male OR female. But the statement is so much more profound than that, because it speaks not only about human gender identity, but about God himself. And that's a biggie.

Read the passage again, but slow down this time, and focus on the last sentence:

So God created mankind in his own image, in the image of God he created them; male and female he created them.

Did you catch it this time? In the image of God he created them, male AND female. It doesn't say "or," it says "and," which tells us *God* is both, and we are not binary.

This may seem like verbal gymnastics, but it truly isn't. Christian LGBTQI+ critics tout the passage as the definitive indictment of non-conforming gender and sexual identities. Biblical literalists demand we take the words to mean what they say. It is only logical that we should therefore examine the words closely, and delve deep into the awesome mystery of God's creation, and of his very being.

The majority of the adult population grew up with traditional concepts of femininity and masculinity, and has associated gender with sex characteristics. Many schools of Christian thought believe we carry a binary gender when we leave our bodies. But when we are no longer equipped with genitalia, Adam's apples, or bone structure, what will our gender resemble? Will our presences in the mystical state known as heaven be intensified versions of binary genders, or will our spirits broaden to be even more like God? More fully *both*, just as God is?

When we allow the Holy Spirit to breathe meaning through today's scripture we make a magnificent discovery:

Gender fluid people are actually more God-like than those who identify with a gender binary.

Deep inside the universe lies the potential of the phenomena of consciousness. The mystery of "you" existed as a potential within the stuff of matter for billions of years, and before that within the infinite sea of consciousness that is God, of which you are a wave. Here you are, birthed out of the ecstatic merging of two others, you are consciousness that learns and grows. You are a child of the universe, a child of the stars, a child of the earth, a child of God, blossomed from love into an infinite love awakening. In all infinite time and possibilities, infinity gave way to you. Here you are.

Jacob. M. Wright

DAY 2: THE COMPLEXITY OF BIOLOGICAL SEX

"Haven't you read," he replied, "that at the beginning the Creator 'made them male and female,'" (Matthew 19:4 NIV)

When Jesus was confronted by Pharisees who tried to trick him with questions about divorce, he quoted a Genesis creation account in order to illustrate the one-ness of spirit which should come about through marriage. But modern day Pharisees use Jesus' words as a demand for a gender binary, which takes the passage out of context and perverts its meaning.

Demanding that God works only in binaries isn't merely sad, it also flies in the face of actual facts. There are at least five scientifically identifiable biological sexes, though Christian traditionalists want to force gender to correspond with only the first two:

1. People who are born with XX chromosomes and have female sex characteristics.
2. People who are born with XY chromosomes and have male sex characteristics.
3. People who are born with XX chromosomes and have male sex characteristics.
4. People who are born with XY chromosomes and have female sex characteristics.
5. People who are born with mosaic genetics, so that some cells contain XX chromosomes and others contain XY. Sexual characteristics for these people vary.

This list is hardly exhaustive. There are also people whose external genitalia appear to be male while the internal organs are female, and vice versa. Brain differences introduce further diversity into the sex and gender spectrum. The presence or absence of testosterone levels during gestation impacts "femininity" and "masculinity" as understood by culture and as understood by the individual themselves.

The result of all this is effulgent diversity.

God created Adam and Eve male and female. Sometimes they create people at the ends of the male/female spectrum. And sometimes they create them in the middle, where the "and" exists.

What's happening outside church walls is happening inside church walls. It is all part of the human experience. Ignorance and lack of education about sex, sexual orientation, gender identities, and human sexuality in general have led to harmful assumptions and poor pastoral counsel.
Kathy Baldock

DAY 3: PRISONERS OF OUR BODIES

The very night before Herod was going to bring him out, Peter, bound with two chains, was sleeping between two soldiers, while guards in front of the door were keeping watch over the prison. Suddenly an angel of the Lord appeared and a light shone in the cell. He tapped Peter on the side and woke him, saying, "Get up quickly." And the chains fell off his wrists. The angel said to him, "Fasten your belt and put on your sandals." He did so. Then he said to him, "Wrap your cloak around you and follow me." Peter went out and followed him; he did not realize that what was happening with the angel's help was real; he thought he was seeing a vision. After they had passed the first and the second guard, they came before the iron gate leading into the city. It opened for them of its own accord, and they went outside and walked along a lane, when suddenly the angel left him. Then Peter came to himself and said, "Now I am sure that the Lord has sent his angel and rescued me from the hands of Herod and from all that the Jewish people were expecting." (Acts 12:6-11 NRSV)

Peter was an ardent Christian who undoubtedly took to heart Jesus' words about taking up the cross and following him. If he thought it was God's will, he probably would have been content to remain in jail, even though prisons of the era must have been terrible places. Peter experienced fully what Paul later described in detail: the honor and glory of sharing in his Lord's sufferings, for God's purposes.

Some Christian denominations are sympathetic to LGBTQI+ realities but believe individuals should deny themselves a life of authenticity. They think this is a cross God placed on their shoulders, and that they will be rewarded for the suffering their denial creates.

But God sent an angel to free Peter.

Peter must have been afraid. Afraid worse pain and perhaps even death waited outside rather than freedom. After all, two guards were assigned to watch over him. Like him, LGBTQI+ individuals are scared of what will happen if they come out of their prisons.

Peter could have remained in his cell, questioning and doubting what the angel meant. He could have argued scrupulously with the angel about his need to participate in the suffering of Christ. What would have happened if he said "no" to the angel? What would have happened if he stayed there, shackled in darkness?

God calls each of us out of our prisons, in different ways, using different angelic voices. Listen for yours. If you don't come out when God calls, he can't use you.

It is better to live one day on the planet being true to yourself than an entire lifetime which is a lie.

Anthony Venn-Brown

DAY 4: LIKE US IN ALL WAYS

Since the children have flesh and blood, he too shared in their humanity so that by his death he might break the power of him who holds the power of death—that is, the devil—and free those who all their lives were held in slavery by their fear of death. For surely it is not angels he helps, but Abraham's descendants. For this reason he had to be made like them, fully human in every way, in order that he might become a merciful and faithful high priest in service to God, and that he might make atonement for the sins of the people. (Hebrews 2:14-17 NIV)

Hebrews is a gorgeous book, filled with rich, liturgical language and deep theological thought. You can almost smell the incense as you read it.

The author reminds us today that Jesus was fully human and like us in all ways. This is a profound thought, and not to be brushed away without examination. If Jesus is like us in all ways, it means he is like us in all our gender and sexual diversity. He is heterosexual, homosexual, bisexual, asexual, male, female, transgender, agender, and intersex. He is every variation imaginable, and then some.

Fully like us.

Fully understanding of all the ways in which our unique set of circumstances pulls us into acts both righteous and foul, having experienced the tug himself.

Jesus is the one in whom you can place your trust, no matter how you identify. Jesus, our non-binary God. Jesus, whose preferred pronouns might be he/him/his, but who we know to be more. Jesus, like you in every way, is the one who will be your judge.

What he's been creating, since the first beat of your heart, is a living, breathing, priceless work of art.
Steven Curtis Chapman

DAY 5: FEARFULLY AND WONDERFULLY MADE

Where can I go from your Spirit? Where can I flee from your presence? If I go up to the heavens, you are there; if I make my bed in the depths, you are there. If I rise on the wings of the dawn, if I settle on the far side of the sea, even there your hand will guide me, your right hand will hold me fast. If I say, "Surely the darkness will hide me and the light become night around me," even the darkness will not be dark to you; the night will shine like the day, for darkness is as light to you. For you created my inmost being; knit me together in my mother's womb. I praise you because I am fearfully and wonderfully made; your works are wonderful, I know that full well. My frame was not hidden from you when I was made in the secret place, I was woven together in the depths of the earth. Your eyes saw my unformed body; all the days ordained for me were written in your book before one of them came to be. (Psalm 139:7-16 NIV)

LGBTQI+ individuals face a lot of criticism about key issues of identity. Gay, lesbian, and bisexual people just want to be able to love who they love and are attracted to. Transgender people just want to live life according to their true gender. Conservative Christians talk about these things as if they are choices and decisions.

But they aren't.

And you know what? God knows it, even if they don't. He knows it because he formed each of us in our mothers' wombs. As Christians we believe God is in charge of our existence from conception on. As Christians we know God doesn't make mistakes. LGBTQI+ individuals were formed uniquely and particularly, with all their strengths, weaknesses, inherent skills and talents, physical attributes, and brain power. Just like everyone else. We can take no credit in the fact that we are fast runners, have pretty eyes, are good at math, or have straight teeth. These are all gifts from the God who formed us in the womb. We also can take no credit for our gender or our sexuality, nor can we be condemned for them.

We didn't choose them. God did.

Know you are fearfully and wonderfully made, just as you are. Know you cannot hide who you are from God, nor do you need to. He doesn't want you to. He is holding you even when you are in darkness, and all your days are written in his book.

God did not create a black and white world of male and female. Creation is not black and white, it is amazingly diverse, like a rainbow, including sexualities and a variety of non-heterosexual expressions of behaviour, affection and partnering occurring in most species, including humans.

Anthony Venn-Brown

DAY 6: THE SUBTLE SHIFTING OF GENDER

When I bring clouds over the earth and the bow is seen in the clouds, I will remember my covenant that is between me and you and every living creature of all flesh. (Genesis 9:14-15, NRSVCE)

After the massive flood which Noah survived by building an ark, God promised his anger would not burn so hot so as to result in total annihilation again. The symbol he created for that promise is a rainbow.

The LGBTQI+ movement chose the rainbow to illustrate the concept of spectrum and variety. But in God's rainbows, there are no distinct demarcations between violet, indigo, blue, and green. The colors gradually shift from one to the next without our ability to detect where one ends and the next begins. The shift between hues is dissolving and soft.

The colors contained within it, the proverbial "all the colors of the rainbow" are only a tiny subset of the hues which other creatures' eyes can see. Our human retinas are limited in their cones and rods. Our human minds are just as limited. Maybe even more so.

God's palette of shifting hues is vast, subtle, and beyond our comprehension.

We humans are like those colors. Subtle, shifting, unique. Non-binary. Unable to be labeled or singled out. Beautiful and one-of-a-kind, and seen by God's eyes alone.

The white light streams down to be broken up by those human prisms into all the colors of the rainbow. Take your own color in the pattern and be just that.
Charles R. Brown

DAY 7: GENDER IDENTIFICATION IN THE TALMUD

When God created mankind, he made them in the likeness of God. He created them male and female and blessed them.
(Genesis 5:1-2 NIV)

Today we look to the Jewish roots of our faith. The Talmud is an ancient collection of 63 tractates which instructed Jews on how to live. One of the tractates talks about the intersection of biological sex and gender performance, and lists these four categories in addition to male and female:

Androgynos: a person whose external sex characteristics are both male and female.

Tumtum: a person whose external sex characteristics are hidden or unclear.

Aylonit: a biological female who hasn't started to look "womanly" by the time she is 20.

Saris: a biological male who hasn't started to look "manly" by the time he is 20.

These descriptions are driven by body parts rather than identity. The system was developed because gender rules for behavior were closely connected to whether a person was biologically male or female. The Old Testament is filled with rules for male and female behavior.

Here's one example for how gender assignment played out:

Blowing a shofar and listening to the sound was an important part of some religious rituals. Males were allowed to blow it for everyone to hear. Androgynos could blow it only for other androgynos to hear. Tumtum could blow it only for themselves to hear.

As with Christianity, most of these rules are no longer followed by many Jewish congregations. But at the time of writing, the Jewish faithful recognized that biological sex and gender were non-binary and had to find a way for non-binary people to know what they could and couldn't do. Judaism is the religion out of which Christianity sprang. It held rules and law to be intrinsically connected to righteousness, yet understood the reality of biological variety. Isn't it odd that our modern version of rules-driven Christianity can't accept that reality?

The more we let God take us over, the more truly ourselves we become – because He made us. He invented us. He invented all the different people that you and I were intended to be.

C.S. Lewis

Sexuality and Marriage
(Week One)

If you've heard it once, you've heard it a million times: "marriage is between one man and one woman." But is this a biblical premise? Is gender really God's primary concern when it comes to matrimony?

Marriages are imploding all around us. Sometimes you can see it coming years ahead of time. Other times it is a surprise. Meanwhile, much of the conservative Christian world sounds the alarm about the destruction of family through gay marriage.

For the next two weeks we explore the Bible's presentation of sexuality and marriage to discover God's vision of loving marital unity. We've saved this section until now, because our understanding of sexuality within a Christian context must be based on all of the other things which came before.

May your hearts and minds be opened by the Holy Spirit to receive what he would give you.

DAY 1: THE SACREDNESS OF SEXUALITY

You seduced me, Lord, and I let myself be seduced; you were too strong for me, and you prevailed. I say I will not mention him, I will no longer speak in his name. But then it is as if fire is burning in my heart, imprisoned in my bones; I grow weary holding back, I cannot!
(Jeremiah 20:7, 9 NABRE)

Much of our contemporary culture views sex as merely a biological function not far removed from urination and defecation, as if it's just a particularly strong itch to be scratched. Many branches of Christianity view sex as something dirty. But to view it either way is grossly out of whack.

Romantic love includes an intense desire for union with the beloved. This desire is a search for completion, for wholeness, and is a reflection of our need for union with God. God gives us this desire for completion with and through other humans because each of us is a reflection of God, and a carrier of God. When we become one with another we are in fact a more complete reflection of God's fullness, though still incomplete. In covenantal union, the two become one as we will eventually become one with Him.

Here's the way our sexual relationships *should* proceed:

First comes love. Out of love comes desire; a desire for union which builds over time. As the relationship grows and deepens, the desire for union also deepens until it becomes a burning gulf between the two, as today's passage from Jeremiah describes. Remaining in the desire becomes a delicious torture, an exquisite torment. This season of restraint and control imprints the couple and changes them. Their bodies, minds, and spirits are changed by the waiting. They are marked by it forever, for each other. Once the time of waiting is fulfilled and they finally come together, the union is sweet beyond words, and pierces the eternal.

In rightly ordered sexuality, we come together covenantally in love. Through the act of lovemaking, there is an intensification of that love, and of passion, pleasure, and joy, which eventually culminates in a great unleashing of force. This reflects God's explosion of love which resulted in creation. God's love, passion, and joy reached such a fever pitch that it exploded in a giant bang, creating matter, energy, light, time, and space.

We are made in the image and likeness of God. Do not underestimate what happens during sex within the context of sacred covenant. It's no wonder the forces of darkness work so hard to corrupt our sexuality. It is the very power of God.

The God of the Bible is not a monistic pudding in which differences are reduced to lumps, or a light that out-dazzles all finite lights and colors. God is a sexual being, the most sexual of all beings....Another reason we are more, not less, sexual in Heaven is that all earthly perversions of true sexuality are overcome, especially the master perversion, selfishness. To make self God, to desire selfish pleasure as the summum bonum, is not only to miss God but to miss pleasure and self as well, and to miss the glory and joy of sex.

Peter Kreeft

DAY 2: SEX OUTSIDE OF MARRIAGE

You have captivated my heart, my sister, my bride; you have captivated my heart with one glance of your eyes, with one jewel of your necklace.
How beautiful is your love, my sister, my bride! How much better is your love than wine, and the fragrance of your oils than any spice!
Your lips drip nectar, my bride; honey and milk are under your tongue; the fragrance of your garments is like the fragrance of Lebanon.
A garden locked is my sister, my bride, a spring locked, a fountain sealed.
Your shoots are an orchard of pomegranates with all choicest fruits, henna with nard, nard and saffron, calamus and cinnamon, with all trees of frankincense, myrrh and aloes, with all choice spices—a garden fountain, a well of living water, and flowing streams from Lebanon.
Awake, O north wind, and come, O south wind! Blow upon my garden, let its spices flow. (Song of Songs 4:9-16 ESV)

Try not to be shocked, but despite the ardent proclamations by legalistic Christians, there's a whole lot of disordered sexuality happening within one man/one woman marriages, and a whole lot of God-ordered sexuality happening outside them.

Marriage is a wonderful, godly institution, but our designer and creator's plan isn't that marriage certificates be issued by a priest or a justice of the peace as a sort of sexual learner's permit. God's will is not that you simply fill out the right paperwork and say the right responses at the proper time, then whoopee: on with the whoopee!

He wants instead for us to recognize the centrality of the act to our design. He wants us to engage in the fullness of our sexuality, and the fullness of anything can only take place in the context of love. Real love, which always has its root in the One who *is* love.

How ravishing is today's passage from the Song of Songs, authored by a guy with hundreds of wives and concubines who bears the title of wisest of all men? How gorgeously ravishing. The book is said to be a sign of the relationship God wants to have with us. He wants to be part of our lovemaking, to be the third strand in an eternal chord. He wants us to understand that our sexuality is one of the ways we are most sacred. He wants us to be one as the persons of the Trinity are one.

Here on earth, sexual union in a sacred context brings us as close to the Trinitarian union as we can temporally achieve. If sexual relations are engaged in outside of that context, they aren't ordered the way God desires them. Disordered sex happens both in and outside of marriage. Marriage is not the key to having sex according to God's design.

Let's pray, for ourselves and all those we love, that we become one only with someone who prays with us before, during, and after acts of love.

Christians throughout history have affirmed that lifelong celibacy is a spiritual gift and calling, not a path that should be forced upon someone.
Matthew Vines

DAY 3: ADAM AND EVE ARE NOT THE OPTIMAL MODEL FOR MARRIAGE

The Lord God said, "It is not good for the man to be alone. I will make a helper suitable for him." So the Lord God caused the man to fall into a deep sleep; and while he was sleeping, he took one of the man's ribs and then closed up the place with flesh. Then the Lord God made a woman from the rib he had taken out of the man, and he brought her to the man.
(Genesis 2:18, 21-22 NIV)

One of the primary Christian arguments against same sex marriage is the Genesis account of human creation. "It was Adam and Eve, not Adam and Steve!" is the adamant refrain. But can that pair *really* be God's image of an ideal marriage?

The first problem with this notion is that Eve seems to be the inauguration of human cloning (though God added a tail to the Y chromosome in the process). Most people agree that mating with our closest genetic match isn't such a great idea, and a number of scriptures decry it. The second problem is that Adam and Eve were the only humans available. They had no one else to pick; it was just them, the animals, and that wicked serpent. In Western cultures, most people believe we should have a say about whom we choose to marry, but Adam and Eve had no choice. The third problem is the pair was immediately dysfunctional. They didn't communicate when temptation arose, they blamed each other for joint mistakes, and just look at what happened to their kids! Lastly, this first couple, who are at the heart of the one-man-one-woman argument, never had what we consider marriage today. Their union may have been sanctioned by God, but it certainly wasn't officiated over by either church or state.

So let's put the whole thing together. If Adam and Eve *are* the optimal model for marriage, Christians who demand a literal interpretation of scripture must conclude the following:

Marriage should be between genetic twins, should not involve choice of partner, should not require civil or ecclesiastic involvement, and should be dysfunctional.

This sounds like a list of everything a marriage should *not* be! But that's okay, because Adam and Eve were never meant to provide a paradigm for marriage. The salvation story as a whole is the model for coupling, culminating in the sacrificial love of Christ. The prototype for marriage centers on fidelity, trust, love, covenant, forgiveness, and generosity. None of those things are demonstrated in the Adam and Eve accounts in Genesis.

Surely Adam and Steve could do better.

From a theological perspective, marriage primarily involves a covenant-keeping relationship of mutual self-giving that reflects God's love for us.
Matthew Vines

DAY 4: "TRADITIONAL" MARRIAGE

This is a faithful saying: If a man desires the position of a bishop, he desires a good work. A bishop then must be blameless, the husband of one wife, temperate, sober-minded, of good behavior, hospitable, able to teach; not given to wine, not violent, not greedy for money, but gentle, not quarrelsome, not covetous; one who rules his own house well, having his children in submission with all reverence (for if a man does not know how to rule his own house, how will he take care of the church of God?); not a novice, lest being puffed up with pride he fall into the same condemnation as the devil. (1 Timothy 3:1-6 NKJV)

You will often hear Christians demand that the Bible says marriage is between one man and one woman. They call this "traditional marriage." But what does "traditional" mean? Most often the word is related to time; the length of a practice and its repetition renders something a tradition. So let's look at the "one man, one woman/traditional marriage" argument from the perspective of time.

Polygynous marriage (one man, more than one woman) was alive and well in Christianity until relatively recently. As you can see from today's passage, it was thriving within the young Christian community, enough so that Paul counseled Bishops to only have *one* wife. This makes it clear polygyny was okay for priests, deacons, and lay people. He didn't condemn having multiple wives in this letter, nor did he in any of the others.

The years marched on, and two doctors of the church—St. Augustine and St. Basil of Caesarea—wrote about the practice without condemnation in the 4th century. Socrates of Constantinople addressed it in the 5th. In the 16th century, Reformation hero Martin Luther proclaimed it permissible under some circumstances, saying:

I confess that I cannot forbid a person to marry several wives, for it does not contradict the Scripture. If a man wishes to marry more than one wife he should be asked whether he is satisfied in his conscience that he may do so in accordance with the word of God. In such a case the civil authority has nothing to do in the matter.

The Council of Trent took a firm stance on the issue in 1563, finally declaring polygyny and concubinage anathema. We'll ignore the polygyny which continues in some Mormon circles and call 1563 the beginning of "one man, one woman." It's been 453 years since then (as of the date of this writing).

Abraham is the first biblical example of polygyny, and he walked the earth around 2,000BCE. That means for at least 3,563 years, marriage between one man and more than one woman was occurring among the faithful. That's 3,563 years of polygyny compared to 453 years of "one man, one woman".

Which, then, is more "traditional?"

The marriage institution cannot exist among slaves, and one sixth of the population of democratic America is denied its privileges by the law of the land. What is to be thought of a nation boasting of its liberty, boasting of its humanity, boasting of its Christianity, boasting of its love of justice and purity, and yet having within its own borders three millions of persons denied by law the right of marriage?

Frederick Douglass

DAY 5: WHAT GOD HAS JOINED TOGETHER

The Pharisees approached and asked, "Is it lawful for a husband to divorce his wife?" They were testing him. He said to them in reply, "What did Moses command you?" They replied, "Moses permitted him to write a bill of divorce and dismiss her." But Jesus told them, "Because of the hardness of your hearts he wrote you this commandment. But from the beginning of creation, 'God made them male and female. For this reason a man shall leave his father and mother [and be joined to his wife], and the two shall become one flesh.' So they are no longer two but one flesh. Therefore what God has joined together, no human being must separate."
(Mark 10:2-9 NABRE)

We talked a bit about the Pharisees trying to trick Jesus into contradicting law about divorce last week. We return now to examine what Jesus is saying in a bit more detail.

When legalistic Christians talk about the "what God has joined together" passage they are generally referring to anyone who is married. According to this view, it applies to every couple who walks into the city clerk's office, gets a marriage license, and stands before a pastor or justice of the peace to receive a certificate of marriage. The corollary of this thinking is that God joins the two together in all of these cases.

This idea is significantly flawed. Sure, God *permits* us to marry whoever we want. After all, we have free will. Our selection of spouse falls within his *permissive* will, but God permits many things, including national disasters and sin. Not all marriages fall under his *ordained* will however. Not all matches are made (literally) in heaven. Let's take, for example, the shotgun wedding of a young girl found to be with child after her daddy caught her serial rapist in the act. Is it really God who is joining the two? Or less horrifying, the strangers who meet during a drunken bender in Las Vegas, and are married in an Elvis chapel. Is that really God? Or the woman who was beaten by her father throughout her childhood and gets married to the man who continues that pattern because her sense of unworthiness feels at home with his abuse. Is the pairing truly of God's design?

These are extreme examples to illustrate the point. More common is our tendency to simply fall in love with the wrong person, and demand God's blessing over our choice. Many, many marriages come as a result of our not listening to the voice of reason and of God, whether it be spoken directly by the Spirit, or indirectly through friends, families, and our own logic.

Just because you are married doesn't mean God joined you together. There is no sin in quitting a marriage which was not brought about through his ordained will.

God is not grieved because of "all the homosexuals." Not in the very least. That's religious people you're thinking of. If God is grieved it's because the beautiful, incomparable message of redemption and grace, the sweet peace of a loving relationship, has been truncated, rerouted into a message of behavior-modification and sin-management.

Susan Cottrell

DAY 6: ONE MAN, ONE WOMAN, MANY SLAVES

Slaves, obey your earthly masters with fear, trembling, and sincerity, as when you obey the Messiah. Do not do this only while you're being watched in order to please them, but be like slaves of the Messiah, who are determined to obey God's will. Serve willingly, as if you were serving the Lord and not merely people, because you know that everyone will receive a reward from the Lord for whatever good he has done, whether he is a slave or free. Masters, treat your slaves the same way. Do not threaten them, for you know that both of you have the same Master in heaven, and there is no favoritism with him. (Ephesians 6:5-9 ISV)

"Bible alone" Christians claim we should turn only to scripture for truth, but then turn around and state "truths" which are not actually found in it. The one man, one woman argument is a prime example. Those words appear nowhere in the Bible. If you point this out to them, you'll get a bunch of clobber passages related to marriage, but none of them actually say one man, one woman.

Our scripture passage for today comes from what is referred to as "Instructions for Christian Households." It opens with counsel for married couples, continues with discussion of children, and concludes with treatment of slaves. The marriage section of the epistle (verses 5:21-33) is one of the texts used to bolster the one man, one woman argument. Modern day Pharisees claim God uses those verses as a legislative mandate for marriage. But if that's the case, how does the same set of Christians deal with today's passage? If verses 5:21-33 legislate marriage today, then verses 6:5-9 legislate slavery today. Their logic means God approves of slavery, and mandates the way slaves and masters should behave.

Hopefully you can see the ridiculousness of the idea. The epistles were written for situations within the cultural context of the day. Slavery existed, but a God of love can't wish it to be perpetuated. Similarly, the marriage laws and customs of the time created monetary and societal gender inequities which no longer exist today. There was a need for legislative intervention because the system was unfair. That need no longer exists; just as legal slavery no longer exists in Western cultures.

It boils down to this: either God's intent through these passages is to mandate and approve of *both* institutions (marriage and slavery) as they existed then, or of neither. It isn't honest to claim it for one institution but not for the other.

Scripture talks a *lot* about marriage and fidelity. It is incredibly important. But if Christians are to believe in the Bible alone, as fundamentalists maintain, they should stick to what it *does* say. What it doesn't say is "one man, one woman."

Far from undermining marriage, gay and lesbian couples seeking marriage for themselves are perhaps the institution's best friends. At a time when marriage is seen as less desirable and less necessary for straight couples, gay and lesbian people are lining up at town halls and church doors to participate in this traditional and long-standing institution.

The Right Reverend Gene Robinson

DAY 7: LET MARRIAGE BE HELD IN HONOR

Let marriage be held in honor by all, and let the marriage bed be kept undefiled; for God will judge fornicators and adulterers.
(Hebrews 13:4 NRSV)

Marriage is a sacred union which weaves two souls into a cord of three strands with God. When God draws couples together into this sacred union, no one should try to separate them, as scripture tells us.

But as we discussed earlier this week, not all marriages are orchestrated by God. Not all of them are holy. A heterosexual marriage is not more holy than a same-sex marriage simply because the couple has differing sex organs.

Let's look at it in concrete terms. Of the two scenarios below, which would the Christian God of love prefer? Which better represents God's desire for holy union?

A heterosexual couple who treats each other with disdain, lies, cheats, and dishonors one another, hides what little light they permit under a bushel, and shows the world marriage is a bitter pill to swallow.

or

A same sex couple who treats each other with respect, lives life together joyfully, mutually commits to truth and fidelity, studies God's word together, worships together, serves their church together, and acts as bearers of light and life, and carriers of the good news.

Obviously not all heterosexual couples fit the first profile, nor all same-sex couples the second. Both types of marriages can be found in both scenarios. But of these two, which holds marriage in honor? Of which type is Jesus more likely to say "Well done?"

Marriage, in its truest sense, is a partnership of equals, with neither exercising dominion over the other, but, rather, with each encouraging and assisting the other in whatever responsibilities and aspirations he or she might have.
Gordon B. Hinckley

Sexuality and Marriage (Week Two)

We know we are made in the image and likeness of God, so isn't it strange that we try to remove sexuality from our understanding of the divine? Sex is arguably the most powerfully driving force in humans. How then can it not, in some way, reflect a part of the reality of God?

We began looking at this issue last week. This week we look more closely at what happens when our fallen nature takes what is beautiful and sacred and tramples it in the dirt. As part of this examination, we will study Sodom and Gomorrah; the story most often used to demand that God hates same-sex relationships.

DAY 1: MARRIAGE AS A RULE OF LOVE

Wives, submit yourselves to your husbands as to the Lord. For the husband is the head of his wife as the Messiah is the head of the church. "That is why a man will leave his father and mother and be united with his wife, and the two will become one flesh." This is a great secret, but I am talking about the Messiah and the church.
(Ephesians 5:22-23, 31-32 ISV)

Ephesians 5 is often cited for the "one man one woman" argument about marriage. But a closer look at the text shows us there's a lot more going on here.

At the time of the letter's writing, marriage was a contractual relationship arrived at through a variety of processes and ritualistic methods. Two Roman marital contracts were used in Ephesus. In the first, a woman and her property remained subject to her father when she married. In the second, she and her property became subject to her husband.

In writing the verses in this letter, Paul clarifies the second form was proper within Christian marriage. Women were to no longer be subject to their fathers, but to their husbands. So Paul wasn't writing proscriptively against same-sex relationships. He was dealing with issues of women as property and their ownership; a concept we moderns reject outright.

Luckily Paul's letter doesn't stop there. At the time, marriage was rarely romantic. Men who demonstrated romantic love for their spouses were viewed as emasculated sissies. Paul attempts to correct this by proclaiming the model of Jesus and instructing that it should change. He said men should *love* their wives.

Paul was doing a big thing in this letter. He strove to move marriage from a legal construct to a sacramental reality. He knew it should be transformed from a set of rules to a rule of love.

In Ephesians 5, Paul calls us back to the sacredness of sexual union within marriage, and reminds us of how God wants us to view our spouses. He calls us to be subject to one another, to be faithful defenders of each other. And above all, to be one as he and the Father are one, in the mystical union of one flesh.

Christian sexual ethics is best advised to keep to the quite simple outline of the New Testament. For this is as unchangeable as the nature of divine love which is become flesh in Christ. This is unalterable because a "greater love" than the one shown to men in Christ is not conceivable, not in any phase of our evolving world. So long as the Christian's heart and mind are spellbound by this humble and totally selfless love, he has in his possession the best possible compass for finding his way in the fog of sexual matters. With the image of this love before him he will not be able to maintain that the ideal of self-giving—of true self-giving, not of throwing oneself in front of people—is unrealistic in our world and impracticable. It demands a very great deal: namely, to subordinate everything to the love which does not seek its own; but it gives a great deal more: namely, the only true happiness. One can use sex, like drugs and alcohol, to maneuver oneself into a state of excited, illusory happiness, but one is merely transporting oneself into momentary states which do not alter one's nature or one's heart. The states fade and disappear, and the heart finds itself emptier and more loveless than before. It is only when the innermost heart of man is opened that the sun of love can penetrate into it.

Hans Urs von Balthasar

DAY 2: EVEN THEIR WOMEN EXCHANGED NATURAL SEXUAL RELATIONS

Because of this, God gave them over to shameful lusts. Even their women exchanged natural sexual relations for unnatural ones. In the same way the men also abandoned natural relations with women and were inflamed with lust for one another. Men committed shameful acts with other men, and received in themselves the due penalty for their error.
(Romans 1:26-27 NIV)

The audience for Paul's epistle is the nascent church in Rome. The gentile population there was used to following multiple gods, many of which demanded all sorts of perverse acts as part of cultic worship. In previous verses Paul recalls the making of idols which look like birds and animals. Paul warns these new Christians to be careful, saying since they now know Jesus, they should not mingle Christian theology with the old ways. Paul draws from his extensive understanding of scripture to convince the population that bad things will happen if they try to mix gods and God.

Paul talks about lusts. Lusting is bad. It's often coupled with coveting, fornication, and adultery. That goes for all humans, regardless of orientation. In Romans 1:24 he talks about the ancient people dishonoring their bodies, which many believe to be a reference to masturbation (an action clearly not limited to homosexuals).

Some translations of verse 27 use the phrase "consumed with passion." God does not want us to be consumed with anything but him. He wants all of our being to focus on him, and our sexuality to be channeled through that relationship.

What Paul doesn't address, nor does any writer in the scriptures, is committed same-sex relationships. Paul warns against out of control passions, and he is quite right. God doesn't want us to be controlled by passions, regardless of whether they are hetero, same-sex, or directed entirely at self.

Paul's warning is real and sound, but modern fundamentalist Christians get one part wrong. The verses do not apply *only* to people with same-sex attraction. They apply to us all.

Those who love desire to share with the beloved. They want to be one with the beloved, and Sacred Scripture shows us the great love story of God for his people which culminated in Jesus Christ.

Pope Benedict XVI

DAY 3: THE WISEST MAN HAD HUNDREDS OF WIVES

King Solomon was greater in riches and wisdom than all the other kings of the earth. The whole world sought audience with Solomon to hear the wisdom God had put in his heart.

King Solomon, however, loved many foreign women besides Pharaoh's daughter—Moabites, Ammonites, Edomites, Sidonians and Hittites. They were from nations about which the Lord had told the Israelites, "You must not intermarry with them, because they will surely turn your hearts after their gods." Nevertheless, Solomon held fast to them in love. He had seven hundred wives of royal birth and three hundred concubines, and his wives led him astray. As Solomon grew old, his wives turned his heart after other gods, and his heart was not fully devoted to the Lord his God, as the heart of David his father had been. The Lord became angry with Solomon because his heart had turned away from the Lord, the God of Israel, who had appeared to him twice.
(1 Kings 10:23-24, and 11:1-4, 9 NIV)

From earlier stories in 1 Kings we know Solomon prayed for God's wisdom, and God honored his prayer. Today's passage reports that King Solomon was greater in wisdom than all the other kings of the earth, and the whole world came to him because of it.

But despite this wisdom, Solomon did not ascribe to the "one man, one woman" model which modern conservative Christians demand as the biblical standard. Quite the opposite; the king had hundreds of wives and a retinue of women with whom he wasn't married. This wisest among men had marital relations with a thousand women, perhaps more.

Is God displeased by the numbers? Does his anger burn hot because Solomon engaged in a one-man, legion-of-women model?

Not according to the biblical account. In these passages, God is not angered because of the numbers, but because the women weren't followers of Yahweh. There is no biblical record that God objected to Solomon's love for multiple women, but it's clear he opposed Solomon's clinging to those who would lead him astray.

And lead him they did.

God desires fidelity. Fidelity within marriage, and especially, fidelity to him. Our lesson in today's readings is that a restrictive model for marriage isn't the point. Fidelity to God is.

Christian discipleship is a decision to walk in his ways, steadily and firmly, and then finding that the way integrates all our interests, passions, and gifts, our human needs and eternal aspirations. It is the way of life we were created for.

Eugene H. Peterson

DAY 4: THE FALSE UNDERSTANDING OF SODOM AND GOMORRAH

The two angels came to Sodom in the evening, and Lot was sitting in the gate of Sodom. When Lot saw them, he rose to meet them and bowed himself with his face to the earth and said, "My lords, please turn aside to your servant's house and spend the night and wash your feet. Then you may rise up early and go on your way." They said, "No; we will spend the night in the town square." But he pressed them strongly; so they turned aside to him and entered his house. And he made them a feast and baked unleavened bread, and they ate. But before they lay down, the men of the city, the men of Sodom, both young and old, all the people to the last man, surrounded the house. And they called to Lot, "Where are the men who came to you tonight? Bring them out to us, that we may know them."
(Genesis 19:1-5 ESV)

Over the next few days we'll explore the sad fate of Sodom and Gomorrah, and debunk the idea that gay sex caused God to send meteors to smash the cities into violent destruction. Let's start with the last sentence in this passage, when the men of the town came and made their first demand that Lot bring out the visiting angels.

If this was a town in which homosexual behavior was so pervasive, why would the men need to come en masse to have sex with the angels? A town full of people doesn't suddenly become so sexually aroused they are overcome and need an outlet. If that was the case, they would simply turn to each other to fulfill their desire. The answer is they weren't there to have run-of-the-mill sex with the angels they believed to be men. They were there to *rape* them.

Rape was an action of violence and power and remains so today. At that time, rape was a sign of victory over an opponent. In this case, it appears the men of the town wished to display their victory over the desires of God for love, mercy, and hospitality. You can almost imagine the demonic horde arriving to face off against the two angels of light, their faces distorted in gleeful anticipation and false triumph.

Despite the horror of this story, it is a wonderful illustration of God's promise in a nutshell. The forces of darkness are in a constant battle to extinguish love, care, protection, and charity. Darkness demands it will be victorious, but God shows darkness will not prevail. He utterly destroys the writhing centers of hate.

We are called to do the same. Not through destruction, but by simply acting like the angels in this story, who later help Lot and his daughters escape. We are to be the presence of God among people even if they don't recognize him.

Oh Lord, become the master of our passions, and the creator of our desires.
R. Marklund

DAY 5: LOT'S DAUGHTERS ARE OFFERED UP

But Lot went out to them at the doorway, and shut the door behind him, and said, "Please, my brothers, do not act wickedly. Now behold, I have two daughters who have not had relations with man; please let me bring them out to you, and do to them whatever you like; only do nothing to these men, inasmuch as they have come under the shelter of my roof."
(Genesis 19:6-8 NASB)

The horde of evil-consumed men froth and lather at Lot's door, demanding the angelic visitors come out so they can gang rape them. Yesterday's reading tells us it was *all of the men* from the city; a veritable sea of diabolical faces. In response, Lot offers his virgin daughters to these monsters.

Many scholars believe the central issue of this story is hospitality. Hospitality was a moral institution driven by the harsh conditions of the region and the nomadic existences of many peoples. If food, water, and shelter were not provided to strangers, they would simply die. Biblical law in Exodus and Leviticus demanded hospitableness, as did simple custom. Given the importance of welcoming and protecting strangers, Lot demonstrates his opposition to the pounding on the door by offering his daughters instead.

But no rational person can comprehend how such an action is righteous. The raping of Lot's daughters was also prohibited by law, not to mention a violation of the simple love between father and child. Women were not permitted to have sexual relations outside of marriage, and yet here we have Lot suggesting it.

Given this reality, if God's anger at Sodom and Gomorrah was driven by sexual misconduct, why was Lot not killed for his willingness to submit his daughters to this violation of law?

Lot must have been so driven by a desire to do what he perceived was right—protecting the visitors—he offered up what he considered a lesser violation. God in his mercy must have judged Lot's intention, despite the sinful horror of his offering.

Maybe [Sodom and Gomorrah] isn't really about homosexuality, but about rape. If the angels had been female, and the men of Sodom said they wanted to 'know' them against their will, would people claim that the story shows heterosexuality is a sin?

Alex Sanchez

DAY 6: LOT'S DAUGHTERS COMMIT INCEST

Then Lot went up out of Zoar and dwelt in the mountains, and his two daughters were with him; for he was afraid to dwell in Zoar. And he and his two daughters dwelt in a cave. Now the firstborn said to the younger, "Our father is old, and there is no man on the earth to come in to us as is the custom of all the earth. Come, let us make our father drink wine, and we will lie with him, that we may preserve the lineage of our father." So they made their father drink wine that night. And the firstborn went in and lay with her father, and he did not know when she lay down or when she arose. It happened on the next day that the firstborn said to the younger, "Indeed I lay with my father last night; let us make him drink wine tonight also, and you go in and lie with him, that we may preserve the lineage of our father." Then they made their father drink wine that night also. And the younger arose and lay with him, and he did not know when she lay down or when she arose. Thus both the daughters of Lot were with child by their father. (Genesis 19:30-36 NKJV)

In this scene, Sodom and Gomorrah have both been destroyed, Lot's wife has been turned into a pillar of salt, and Lot and his daughters are living away from the broken humanity which resulted in such trauma and tragedy.

What happens next? Lot's daughters undertake actions which are yet *another* violation of God's law; they commit incest. Not only that, they rape their father by getting him so drunk he doesn't know enough to stop them.

If God's wrath upon the two cities was based on sexual immorality, why were these two females spared? God is outside of time and knew what was to come. Even as he sat talking with Abraham about the number of righteous in Sodom and Gomorrah, he pictured these two sinners, violating their father sexually.

When you look at the entirety of the picture, it's impossible to conclude the towns were destroyed because of homosexual behavior by the townspeople.

It simply wasn't about sex.

But as I became more aware of same-sex relationships, I couldn't understand why they were supposed to be sinful, or why the Bible apparently condemned them. With most sins, it wasn't hard to pinpoint the damage they cause. Adultery violates a commitment to your spouse. Lust objectifies others. Gossip degrades people. But committed same-sex relationships didn't fit this pattern. Not only were they not harmful to anyone, they were characterized by positive motives and traits instead, like faithfulness, commitment, mutual love, and self-sacrifice.

Matthew Vines

DAY 7: ISAIAH AND EZEKIEL ON SODOM AND GOMORRAH

Hear the word of the Lord, you rulers of Sodom; listen to the instruction of our God, you people of Gomorrah! "The multitude of your sacrifices— what are they to me?" says the Lord. "I have more than enough of burnt offerings, of rams and the fat of fattened animals; I have no pleasure in the blood of bulls and lambs and goats. Stop bringing meaningless offerings! Your incense is detestable to me. When you spread out your hands in prayer, I hide my eyes from you; even when you offer many prayers, I am not listening. Your hands are full of blood! Wash and make yourselves clean. Take your evil deeds out of my sight; stop doing wrong. Learn to do right; seek justice. Defend the oppressed. Take up the cause of the fatherless; plead the case of the widow. "Come now, let us settle the matter," says the Lord. "Though your sins are like scarlet, they shall be as white as snow; though they are red as crimson, they shall be like wool. If you are willing and obedient, you will eat the good things of the land; but if you resist and rebel, you will be devoured by the sword." For the mouth of the Lord has spoken. (Isaiah 1:10-11, 13, 15-20 NIV)

"Now this was the sin of your sister Sodom: She and her daughters were arrogant, overfed and unconcerned; they did not help the poor and needy." (Ezekiel 16:49 NIV)

Sodom and Gomorrah are used more than any other Bible story to admonish people about same-sex relationships. The fact that a crowd of men pounded on Lot's door and demanded to rape the visiting angels has become the rallying cry for why men should not love men, and women should not love women. We've discussed how the citizens' actions were a violation of the enshrined and crucial hospitality customs which ensured the survival of nomadic people and of travelers. But that reality isn't enough to dissuade conservative Christians about the meaning of the destruction of the cities.

But do not despair; today's passages will serve you well the next time someone offers you that tarnished old argument. The first comes from Isaiah, harbinger of Jesus and remonstrator of the perpetually unfaithful followers of God. The prophet of prophets one might even say. What does Isaiah tells us about Sodom and

Gomorrah? Does he talk about sexual behavior? No. Not even once. Isaiah warns us not to be like the people of those cities because they did not seek justice, defend the oppressed, care for the fatherless, and help the widow. He says it doesn't matter how closely we adhere to the law with all its rules about sacrifice and prayer, if we aren't doing justice. Ezekiel chimes in with the same message.

Today's conservative Christians can perform all sorts of pious practices which replaced the burning fat of rams from Isaiah's day. They can memorize Bible passages, tithe, and preach on street corners until their throats are sore. But without mercy and justice, they are like Isaiah's audience, which the Lord compares to the sinners of Sodom and Gomorrah.

Our misery is that we thirst so little for these sublime things, and so much for the mocking trifles of time and space.
Charles H. Spurgeon

WHAT DOES IT TAKE TO
GET TO HEAVEN?

Socially conservative Christians often make claims about why LGBTQI+ individuals will not make it into heaven. They say the scriptures are clear on this issue. During this last week of devotions together we examine what the Bible actually says about what it takes to be saved. The descriptions are many, varied, and often contradictory, which is why we *must* rely on the loving acceptance of he who is love and mercy itself.

DAY 1: FOR GOD SO LOVED THE WORLD

For God so loved the world, that he gave his only Son, that whoever believes in him should not perish but have eternal life. (John 3:16 ESV)

We begin our meditations on the requirements for salvation with these electrifying words from the beloved disciple. Perhaps you've heard them so often they've come to sound trite or meaningless. But we start here because this single sentence contains the whole of the Good News: "...whoever believes in him should not perish but have eternal life."

"Whoever" is not qualified in any way. It doesn't say "whoever loves him but is without sin," or "whoever loves him and tithes 10%," or "whoever loves him and is cisgender." The term "whoever" stands alone.

Let's also look at the sentences which follow this verse:

For God did not send his Son into the world to condemn the world, but in order that the world might be saved through him. Whoever believes in him is not condemned.

Jesus addresses these statements to Nicodemus, who is referred to as a ruler of the Jews. Nicodemus came to question Jesus about how a person could be born again. Jesus chastises him because as a teacher of Israel, Nicodemus should have been able to understand. But he could not, or would not. Nicodemus is a prefigurement of today's fundamentalist Christians who have similar trouble.

John summarizes things for us so beautifully. First he says "In the beginning was the Word, and the Word was with God, and the Word was God." Then he tells us "For God so loved the world that he gave his only Son, that *whoever* believes in him should not perish but have eternal life."

Simple. Powerful. Inclusive. True.

Jesus Christ came not to condemn you but to save you, knowing your name, knowing all about you, knowing your weight right now, knowing your age, knowing what you do, knowing where you live, knowing what you ate for supper and what you will eat for breakfast, where you will sleep tonight, how much your clothing cost, who your parents were. He knows you individually as though there were not another person in the entire world. He died for you as certainly as if you had been the only lost one. He knows the worst about you and is the One who loves you the most.

A.W. Tozer

DAY 2: NOT EVERYONE WHO SAYS LORD, LORD...

Not everyone who says to me, 'Lord, Lord,' will enter the kingdom of heaven, but only the one who does the will of my Father in heaven. On that day many will say to me, 'Lord, Lord, did we not prophesy in your name, and cast out demons in your name, and do many deeds of power in your name?' Then I will declare to them, 'I never knew you; go away from me, you evildoers.' (Matthew 7:21-23 NRSV)

This is the second-to-last instruction in Jesus' powerful Sermon on the Mount. Prior to these words, he outlines what it means to be his follower, and what it takes to do the Father's will. Instructions are given regarding doing good works, offering forgiveness, loving our neighbors, trusting in God's provision, not showing off your piety, not judging, doing unto others, and evaluating the fruits of contemporary prophets.

All of these things are the will of the Father which Jesus mentions in today's passage. Nowhere in this sermon, a speech so long it takes three chapters to cover, does Jesus mention slavish adherence to law. Quite the opposite; chapter 5 verses 17-20 describe Jesus' fulfillment of the law and the impossibility of righteousness through the methods of the scribes and Pharisees. In verses 21-48 of the same chapter, Jesus offers a series of comparisons of what the scriptures told the Jewish people to do versus what *he* was now telling them to do. So it's pretty clear the will of the Father of which Jesus spoke was not about adherence to law.

This leads us to the inevitable conclusion that those very scribes and Pharisees, the ones who strain gnats out of water so as not to be defiled but ignore the weightier matters of justice and mercy (Matthew 23:23), are the ones Jesus describes crying "Lord, Lord."

The will of the Father is presented through the person and the counsel of Jesus Christ. Listen to *him*.

Thus if you have really handed yourself over to Him, it must follow that you are trying to obey Him. But trying in a new way, a less worried way. Not doing these things in order to be saved, but because He has begun to save you already. Not hoping to get to Heaven as a reward for your actions, but inevitably wanting to act in a certain way because a first faint gleam of Heaven is already inside you.

C.S. Lewis

DAY 3: EVALUATION BY THE JUST JUDGE

Very truly I tell you, a time is coming and has now come when the dead will hear the voice of the Son of God and those who hear will live. For as the Father has life in himself, so he has granted the Son also to have life in himself. And he has given him authority to judge because he is the Son of Man.

"Do not be amazed at this, for a time is coming when all who are in their graves will hear his voice and come out—those who have done what is good will rise to live, and those who have done what is evil will rise to be condemned. By myself I can do nothing; I judge only as I hear, and my judgment is just, for I seek not to please myself but him who sent me.
(John 5:25-30 NIV)

What does the term "judgment" mean?

The judge hears the facts of the case as presented by the accuser and the defendant, and then evaluates the evidence. Judging requires evaluation. At the time of our judgment, our lives will be evaluated. Our motives, our sorrows, our pressing needs, our weaknesses; all the messy mix of good and evil which make up the length of our years.

God's judgement is not binary, like an on/off switch in which you say the sinner's prayer and are in, or make love to someone of the same sex and are out. Binary issues don't require judgment. But over and over again the scriptures speak to us of judgment. And that requires analysis and a deep understanding of each situation.

We have Jesus as our judge. We don't have a particular verse in the Bible as our judge, or even the whole collection of books which make it up. We have a person, who is Love. He alone is our judge, and he does actual judging. Seek to please him, as John advises.

And it is the Lord, it is Jesus, Who is my judge. Therefore I will try always to think leniently of others, that He may judge me leniently, or rather not at all, since He says: "Judge not, and ye shall not be judged."
Thérèse de Lisieux

DAY 4: SHEEP AND GOATS

"When the Son of Man comes in His glory, and all the holy angels with Him, then He will sit on the throne of His glory. All the nations will be gathered before Him, and He will separate them one from another, as a shepherd divides his sheep from the goats. And He will set the sheep on His right hand, but the goats on the left. Then the King will say to those on His right hand, 'Come, you blessed of My Father, inherit the kingdom prepared for you from the foundation of the world: for I was hungry and you gave Me food; I was thirsty and you gave Me drink; I was a stranger and you took Me in; I was naked and you clothed Me; I was sick and you visited Me; I was in prison and you came to Me.' 'Assuredly, I say to you, inasmuch as you did it to one of the least of these My brethren, you did it to Me.'

"Then He will also say to those on the left hand, 'Depart from Me, you cursed, into the everlasting fire prepared for the devil and his angels: for I was hungry and you gave Me no food; I was thirsty and you gave Me no drink; I was a stranger and you did not take Me in, naked and you did not clothe Me, sick and in prison and you did not visit Me.' 'Assuredly, I say to you, inasmuch as you did not do it to one of the least of these, you did not do it to Me.' And these will go away into everlasting punishment, but the righteous into eternal life."
(Matthew 25:31-36, 40-43, 45-46 NKJV)

Today's passage is long, and in it, Jesus describes the way we will be judged. It requires no great skill in exegesis, no training in Greek or even a study of the culture of the day. It is quite clear.

Jesus doesn't say his judgment will be based on how many verses of scripture we can quote, or how many Wednesday nights we spend at church. It doesn't mention what denomination we should go to, or who we can marry, or what kinds of clothes match which external sex characteristics. It breaks his whole message down into how we perform love in the world around us. How we act as the hands and feet and mouth of God to those around us, and by doing so, how we offer him love as well.

If we persecute a trans woman of color and leave her bleeding on the street, as untouchable as the beaten Samaritan Jesus describes in another parable, we leave Christ himself there. If we kick a teenage son out of our home when he announces he can't pretend he isn't gay anymore, we put Christ himself out.

Jesus tells us this story of the judging king so we know what it is we will be judged on.

Jesus is that judging king.

At the evening of life, we shall be judged on our love.
St. John of the Cross

DAY 5: RIGHTEOUSNESS THROUGH FAITH

For the promise to Abraham or to his descendants that he would be heir of the world was not through the Law, but through the righteousness of faith. For if those who are of the Law are heirs, faith is made void and the promise is nullified; for the Law brings about wrath, but where there is no law, there also is no violation. In hope against hope he believed, so that he might become a father of many nations according to that which had been spoken, "So shall your descendants be." Therefore it was also credited to him as righteousness. (Romans 4:13-15, 18, 22 NASB)

Abraham is the father of Christianity, as well as that of Judaism and Islam. When the story described in today's passage took place, Abraham was elderly, yet believed God's promise that his offspring would be as numerous as the stars in heaven or the sands of the seashore.

The essential reality of Christ's coming is summed up in today's passage and tomorrow's. Our relationship with God is not through the law. After the exodus, Moses instituted a rigid structure of edicts and rules. From then on, the faithful believed our connection with God could only be maintained through elaborate and strict adherence to them. But here we have Abraham being held up as the very epitome of righteousness, not because he performed the proper sacramental actions, and not because he was sinless. Scripture shows us he was just as flawed as we are. But his deep, abiding faith in God's promises is what counted.

His *faith* was credited to him as righteousness.

Our righteousness does not come through slavish adherence to law, nor to some impossible ideal of sinlessness. Our righteousness, like Abraham's, comes only through faith.

Faith means the fundamental response to the love that has offered itself up for me. It thus becomes clear that faith is ordered primarily to the inconceivability of God's love, which surpasses us and anticipates us. Love alone is credible; nothing else can be believed, and nothing else ought to be believed. This is the achievement, the 'work' of faith: to recognize this absolute prius, which nothing else can surpass; to believe that there is such a thing as love, absolute love, and that there is nothing higher or greater than it.

Fr. Hans Urs Von Balthasar

DAY 6: WHOEVER CALLS ON THE NAME OF THE LORD SHALL BE SAVED

For the scripture saith, Whosoever believeth on him shall not be put to shame. For there is no distinction between Jew and Greek: for the same Lord is Lord of all, and is rich unto all that call upon him: for, Whosoever shall call upon the name of the Lord shall be saved.
(Romans 10:11-13 ASV)

We've reached the end of this devotional, but the Good News continues.

In his letter to the church in Rome, Paul addresses the spiritual pride of the Jewish followers. It would have been easy for them to look down on the pagan Greeks for not sharing the religious heritage from which Jesus was born. Their polytheism, dietary habits, and understanding of sexuality and gender all would have been cause for disdain.

It wasn't really the Jews' fault. They believed righteousness came through the law, and through the many scriptural injunctions about avoiding interaction with those outside the twelve tribes of Israel. They had very good religious precedent for the kind of discrimination which was lodged in their hearts and minds.

But Paul steps in to correct them. He says there is no difference between Jew and Greek. There was no call for Jewish believers to feel superior or more righteous. He reminds them, and our conservative Christian brothers and sisters today, that the Lord is the Lord of us all, and his promises are given to all who call upon him.

So call upon him.

Certainly all virtues are very dear to God, but humility pleases Him above all the others, and it seems that He can refuse it nothing.
Francis de Sales

177

CONCLUSION

For now we see in a mirror, dimly, but then we will see face to face. Now I know only in part; then I will know fully, even as I have been fully known. (1 Corinthians 13:12, NRSVCE)

Many Christians claim God can be known through the Bible. This 1 Corinthians passage shows the falseness of that idea, but it also declares the promise of a future of intimate revelation about the creator of the cosmos. And there is only one way to get there: through the death of our bodies.

Death is the process by which all our filters for perception are removed, when instead of losing contact with creation we are finally able to perceive it as it truly is, on all levels. From electric hazes of energy to swirling microorganisms to the magnetic pull of atomic structures. We will experience a cosmic give and take, exchanges of oxygen and consumption, of rotting and growth and feeding, of colors undreamt of by our limited cones and rods. We will see smells and lie down on a moving bed of cilia.

Perhaps we will watch our bodies decompose and dance with joy at the transformation of matter and energy. Dancing to the song of birds and the roaring of rivers and blood, the percussion of hearts and particles reforming, the silent sound of planets spinning and the burning of the stars.

In death, when our physicality is stripped away and our essence released to join the eternal song of creation, there is no sin or offense, no judgment or worry. It won't matter how many times we lied or how many commandments we broke, if we slept with 400 men or the single, perfect girl. All of that is meaningless in the majesty of the vast, molecular moment. In this state of being there can be no separation from God, each other, or the universe.

Remember this as you judge one another. Remember who created you, who judges you, and who will soon be united with you in this ultimate consummation of being.

And remembering, go into the world and share the good news.

Made in the USA
Middletown, DE
07 May 2019